DANGEROUS JESUS

FAITH
GOSPEL
CITIZEN
JUSTICE
LOVE
FRIENDSHIPS
BLESSINGS
JOY
SPEECH
SPIRIT
CHRISTIAN

We are in dire need of authors who will write brave, truth-filled books. KB is one of those writers. Few voices are as courageous, clear, relevant, and necessary as his. In a world that seeks to water down the gospel and sugarcoat its Christ, his words provide a critical compass pointing us back home. The volume you are holding in your hands is personal and powerful. Once I started reading, I could not stop. Each chapter unveils the caricature that culture has painted of our Savior and presents a rich reminder of who He truly is—a revolutionary who challenged systems, shifted culture, and inaugurated a new paradigm for living. KB's vulnerability, humility, and theological acumen shimmer on these pages. And, in the end, he extends to his readers an invitation to dive deeper into the surrendered life, which is an abundant life. Read this book slowly, prayerfully, and with holy expectation.

PRISCILLA SHIRER, bestselling author and Bible teacher

KB is one of the most poignant and unique voices of our time. He finds a way to weave unapologetic truth into relatable stories that shine a light on the goodness of God.

LECRAE, Grammy-winning recording artist and *New York Times* bestselling author

KB has issued a powerful call for us to meet the real Jesus and be changed by him. *Dangerous Jesus* is a book soaked in Scripture with an eye towards the pressing concerns of the culture, especially those issues driving young believers away from the faith and hindering skeptics from considering the claims of Jesus. In this book he has done work needed in every age: to scrape away the lies and distortions the culture (and sometimes even, sadly, elements of the church) tells us about the Messiah Jesus so as to be challenged by a God that demands our allegiance.

ESAU McCAULLEY, PhD, author of *Reading While Black* and associate professor at Wheaton College

With an eagle-eye's view, KB locates the core problem areas with contemporary Christianity. Not only does he rightly assess ways we've drifted, but he astutely systematizes the way back to a healthy expression of our beloved faith. Follow KB's words back to the Jesus of Scripture.

FLAME, Grammy-nominated hip-hop artist

Ever since Jesus walked this earth, you had everyone from laymen, bureaucrats, and even the religious establishment seeking to appropriate Him and His influence for their own purposes and interests—painting Him as the paragon of their own cause. However, Jesus never gave Himself over to any to be used in such a way; His Kingdom ethic and mission always transcended man's attempts to conflate Him with their own selfish ends. In his amazing debut book, KB helps us understand what it means to not only see Jesus aright but to live for Him in such a way that aligns our goals and vision with His will. This work will help guide us to not only love Christ with a pure heart but to also sacrificially love our neighbor as we love ourselves, encouraging us to bring a true representation of heaven to the public square.

AMEEN HUDSON, writer, speaker, and cohost of the *Southside Rabbi* podcast

I've had the privilege of knowing KB since he was in his early twenties, freshly signed to Reach Records and still finding his voice. His evolution from rapper to thought leader and author has been nothing short of spectacular. His demeanor is always humble, and his voice is always full of grace and truth. *Dangerous Jesus* is an extension of ideas KB has shared with me over the years, and I'm so excited that the general public is tuning in. I believe this is work that will shape the culture around Christianity for decades to come.

RUSLAN, hip-hop artist, entrepreneur, and content creator

Jesus has been wrongly portrayed by many in society, and sadly, even in the pulpit. That misconception has led many away from the faith. In this book, KB reintroduces us to what the Bible says about Jesus. A fierce yet loving Savior who desires a walk with you that will radically change your life.

TOVARES GREY, founder and author of *Godly Dating 101*

DANGEROUS JESUS

DANGEROUS JESUS

Why the only thing more risky than
getting Jesus right is getting Jesus wrong

KEVIN "KB" BURGESS

TYNDALE
MOMENTUM®

A Tyndale nonfiction imprint

Visit Tyndale online at tyndale.com.

Visit Tyndale Momentum online at tyndalemomentum.com.

Tyndale, Tyndale's quill logo, *Tyndale Momentum*, and the Tyndale Momentum logo are registered trademarks of Tyndale House Ministries. Tyndale Momentum is a nonfiction imprint of Tyndale House Publishers, Carol Stream, Illinois.

Dangerous Jesus: Why the Only Thing More Risky than Getting Jesus Right Is Getting Jesus Wrong

Designed by Dean H. Renninger

Edited by Jonathan Schindler

Published in association with the literary agency of The Fedd Agency, Inc., P.O. Box 341973, Austin, TX 78734.

For information about special discounts for bulk purchases, please contact Tyndale House Publishers at csresponse@tyndale.com, or call 1-855-277-9400.

Library of Congress Cataloging-in-Publication Data

A catalog record for this book is available from the Library of Congress.

ISBN 978-1-4964-5948-0

Printed in China

29	28	27	26	25	24	23
7	6	5	4	3	2	1

I DEDICATE THIS BOOK TO THE ONES SEARCHING FOR JESUS AND
THOSE WHO HAVE FOUND HIM BUT ARE GROWING
WEARY OF HIS MISREPRESENTATIONS.

CONTENTS

Somewhere along the way we traded following Jesus for creating a tame, moldable, silent Jesus who doesn't mind following us.

The church's waning influence on the culture is directly connected to Jesus' waning influence on the church.

Allow me to reintroduce this Jesus.

To recast Christianity in a land of so many misrepresentations makes the truth sound like a reinterpretation.

But dangerous impostors will give way to what's more dangerous: the real Jesus.

KB

FOREWORD

I have one story to share. It's a dangerous one, I suppose. I learned about it in a car ride through Nashville while being driven by a woman that could've been a martyr. She and her family were new transplants to the city after living as missionaries for twenty-plus years in Istanbul, Turkey. I wanted to know the differences between the Christians here, as in America, and the Christians there, as in Turkey, so I asked. She answered with a story about Easter.

Anti-Christian groups were threatening to storm certain churches on Easter Sunday with their weapons and their rage. Upon arrival, they would put bullets in every baptized body. One of the congregations under threat included my Nashville friend, her husband, and her two children.

They all gathered one night to discuss the danger. The weapons. The organized rage headed their way. Naturally fear was felt, and as it usually does, it instigated them into being strategic. The easiest strategy was to simply stay home on Sunday. If on that day, when the sun rose and after breakfast was made, nobody decided to change out of their pajamas and into their best, head to the church, and await the word, then nobody would be there when the rage arrived.

Nobody's body would catch a bullet in it. No child would lose a parent. No parent would lose a child. No spouse would weep and no friend would mourn.

Staying home was an easy tactic—a safe and compelling one for my Nashville friend, in fact—but if my friend wanted a safe Christianity, she would've stayed in the States. So she did what Moses, Daniel, Paul, and especially Jesus did when danger seemed to be the only option available. She prayed. While in that divine space between the natural world and the throne of God, she sensed a reminder. She remembered what *this* Sunday represented and how it didn't involve bunnies and eggs and hunts and pastel dresses and shiny white shoes. *This* Sunday was the communal celebration of a condescended God, wrapped in flesh, Whose body died on a cross and rose from the dead. Then, as she considered the men threatening to bring their guns into her church and what that might mean for her own body and the bodies she wanted to remain alive, she sensed the Spirit of God say, *Do you* really *believe in the Resurrection?* The all-wise God, through His Spirit, unveiled the irony. Resurrection Sunday has *always* been a dangerous one.

At the bottom of every fear is the contemplation of some form of death, death of control or death of life. Either way, to face the fear of death, one must believe that by dying, I am gaining, the ultimate gain being the resurrection of the body. To *truly* believe in the Resurrection for my friend meant to submit to the end of life as she knew it. By doing so, she was transcending the boring and typical tactics of Christians who quote verses regarding the Resurrection in their Instagram captions, cross-legged on their sofas, while refusing to die to self, sin, and safety.

My friend and her family decided against the "Christianity of the Land," as KB calls it. They chose to embody the Christianity of those lauded in Hebrews 11, "who through faith conquered kingdoms, enforced justice, obtained promises, stopped the mouths of lions, quenched the power of fire, escaped the edge of the sword, were made strong out of weakness, became mighty in war, put foreign armies to flight."[1] It is a dangerous thing to really believe the Bible.

They showed up to church that morning and scanned the room. Every single member of the congregation was there, ready to sing or die. In their case, either way was worship. No rage came though. No weapons were drawn. No bullets were scattered. Yet those saints were ready to be like their Jesus on that Resurrection Sunday.

Stories like this are inspiring and yet distant. Most of us aren't in a position to be martyred on a Sunday, but that doesn't mean we aren't under the constant threat of danger because of our faith. Not merely because of cultural and interpersonal antagonism but simply put, Christianity is a threat to our own selves first and foremost. The fundamental nature of the call to follow Jesus is preceded by the command to "leave everything" and "take up your cross and die."

Everything we believe gives us life, love, identity, security, and sanity is threatened when Jesus shows up. No wonder we try to bring it all with us as we go. But Jesus will not and cannot allow you to love both Him and idols. Your heart is His, and by no means will He let you share your affections with a lesser love. That's scary, ain't it? When you look around and see all the shiny little things you think will make you whole and realize that to have God, you and all your little messiahs have to die? But do you *really* believe in the Resurrection—not simply that it inaugurates the resurrection of the body but that it validates the preeminence of the Son, and that if He has power over life and death, then surely He is better than everything that lives? To have Him is to have life, and power, and freedom, and joy. Put your little trinkets next to Jesus, and tell me who's more glorious. Jesus is a threat to your idols, and you, my friend, are a danger to your own self. But *be that*. There is a cross set aside for you to take up, and as heavy as it is, it is the only real way to live.

I applaud you though. To pick up this book, after reading its title and still deciding to engage with its content, you have to have some level of bravery in you. Some propensity for danger. I've come to see that KB is good at that. At making swords approachable. If you haven't noticed this already, it's all through his music. Every song cuts and never coddles, but because it moved you to dance, or sing, or jump, or shadowbox with nothing or someone, you sang a dangerous song out loud without flinching. This work is the same, but beware: there's no music underneath the cutting to make it more palatable. No bass to move you, but trust me, this will move you still. Towards Jesus first. Towards people second. Away from yourself and into a better version that is ready to die to the easy Christianity that's popular. This book is a land mine, a double-edged sword, a cultural critique and theological commentary. KB has the pen of a writer and the heart of a shepherd. He, like my friend in Nashville, believes the Bible, and I don't know if there's anything in the world more dangerous than that.

Jackie Hill Perry
Author, poet, Bible teacher, and hip-hop artist

THE MOST DANGEROUS MAN I EVER MET

No chains on me.

"NO CHAINS"

This is a story about the most dangerous man I ever met.

It starts with me, at fifteen years old, standing frozen in the hallway at my grandmother's house.

My mother and I, fleeing an ugly divorce, had found shelter there. My grandfather, a direct descendant of a slave, was all too familiar with the unkind world his daughters would be thrust into, so he built that house, should his babies ever need it, to serve as a net of safety, restart, and redemption. It was his dream.

But his dream felt more like a nightmare to me because of the constant conflict that surrounded me there.

In this particular incident, my mom and my female cousin were engaged in a full-on MMA-style grappling session on the floor. I would never have even *thought* about challenging my mother—or any of my elders, for that matter—yet here, in reality-TV fashion, my cousin was on top of my mother, trying to hurt her. Their relationship had been a powder keg since we moved in, but this was the first time things had gotten physical. And I simply had no category for what I was seeing.

It started off as a war of words, but then my cousin took things too far, and my mom was never one to tolerate disrespect from children. My cousin wasn't exactly a child—she was older and bigger than me, and her boyfriend was a feared man. But the argument escalated quickly, and before I knew it, my mom and my cousin were on the floor, swinging, clawing, and wrestling, my cousin shouting obscenities and my mom trying with all her might to restrain her.

I just stood in the doorway of my room, unable to move. I had never felt more like a coward. I was the only man in the house, and all I could think was, *I wish Dad were here.* He always knew what to do. I had never even been in a fistfight before. I'd never had to be.

For the past seven years, we had been living on Scott Air Force Base in southern Illinois, where my dad was stationed, and it was objectively one of the safest places in the world. Every day I saw armed soldiers with guns bigger than me protecting every side of our community. In fact, with the exception of seeing a high schooler smoking a cigarette, I cannot recall a single crime ever being committed. There was a police unit on the base, but I never saw them, because there was "nothing to see here."

Even beyond the security of living with soldiers, my dad was there, and I was confident that my dad could beat up your dad, and anybody else your dad came with. I distinctly remember my dad comparing his biceps to mine. I was overwhelmed with the thought that this guy might actually be a superhero. He was my courage.

But after my parents split up, that was gone. The divorce didn't only cost me a father; it cost me my security.

My grandmother's house was located on the south side of St. Petersburg, Florida, which was a very different place from when my grandfather built that house decades ago. The new south side was marked by abject poverty, food insecurity, gang violence, and vulnerability. My existence had become the great exchange—security for insecurity, safety for exposure, and military soldiers for street soldiers.

I heard gunshots nightly. I saw people running from the police and getting into shoot-outs. I remember there was a hurricane once, and the power went out all over the city. In the hood, we were typically the last people to get our power turned back on, so we were without power for what felt like an eternity. Since we couldn't watch TV, we would just sit in the living room and watch whatever was happening outside. We would see drug deals, arguments, and fistfights. I remember one dude waving a pistol in the air, screaming at the top of his lungs, "I'll kill anybody on this block!" It was like watching *Cops* without a cable subscription. It felt like a war zone.

It landed extra scary on me, but most people living there were good, hardworking, honest people. It's the 99 percent that are terrorized by the 1 percent, which is then compounded by the media's tendency to focus on the 1 percent. And even the dope boys and troublemakers making up that 1 percent are a complicated bunch. Some people are just put in situations where they are tempted to make decisions they would never make if they had more stability. Hunger breeds theft. Theft breeds violence. Violence breeds a record. A record keeps you from earning a legitimate income. Lack of income breeds hunger, and we are back where we started. When people are trying to survive, they get desperate. Desperation is dangerous.

I felt *weak*. Back then, I was 110 pounds soaking wet with construction boots on. All around me people were getting shot and jumped, and I knew it was only a matter of time before somebody came for me. Every morning I woke up grateful that I didn't get killed the night before.

Now, I just stood there, helpless, while my mom—my last line of defense against the outside world—was getting attacked by her own flesh and blood. My cousin broke free from Mom's grip, scrambled to her feet, and screamed over my mom, "I'm going to get my boyfriend to kill you! Don't be surprised if he's waiting for you when you get in your car in the morning!"

In that moment, something flipped in my mind. I realized, *It's go time. I've got to be the man of the house. I've got to protect my mom.*

But I had no idea how. I had a switchblade that I bought off one of my cousins, but there are obvious limitations that come with a knife. For one thing, you've got to get in real close to use it, and like I said, I wasn't what you would call an imposing figure. I thought about pepper spray, but I was sure I'd get laughed off the block if I pulled that out. All roads to bona fides seemed to point to getting my hands on a gun. A gun is power. The issue of walking home from school or defending my mother—and, quite frankly, being a man in general—would be instantly solved. It was as if the clouds had opened and the panacea I so desperately desired appeared in the shape of a 9 mm handgun.

In all that was falling apart around me, school was the only thing that came easy to me. I don't know if I was gifted or simply killing it at a failing school, but my GPA qualified me for a pilot program that allowed me to start college at age fifteen. I shortly found myself taking classes with adults.

I became friends with one guy that I would play basketball with after class. He was one of those guys that could get their hands on anything. And by anything, I mean *anything.* Everybody in the hood knows a guy like this. From fake IDs to DVDs of movies that hadn't even come out yet, he was the plug. Often after we finished playing ball, we would do a little gambling. I'd have my lunch money, and he would wager things like sneakers or throwback jerseys—whatever he had that could serve as currency.

The game of choice was called quarters. We'd flip the quarter, somebody would call out heads or tails, and whoever got it right would win. We had been playing long enough that we were raising the stakes beyond the money we had with us, so I rested the quarter on the back of my thumb, and before I flipped it, I said, "So what else you got?"

He sat back and thought about it for a second. Then he said, "I got this gun at home. It's not a real gun. It's one of those Airsoft guns that shoots BBs. But it looks just like a real one. It won't kill you, but if you get shot with it, it will break the skin."

I thought, *Man, there must be a God—this is exactly what I need!* It was the best of both worlds. That gun would offer the threat of a real gun but without the lethal capacity and subsequent incarceration that comes along with it. Of course, I wasn't factoring into my mind that I would be pulling a fake gun on people that had real guns, but in my mind, the aesthetic was king, and I'd cross that other bridge when I got there.

I was all in. I put up my sneakers and gleefully shouted, "Let's get it!" Then I flipped the quarter. "Call it."

"Tails."

I caught the quarter in my right hand and slapped it onto the back of my left.

"Heads!"

He slumped back and cursed under his breath. Then he looked at me. "I'll bring it on Friday."

Man, I was lit. I mean, this was it. I was finally going to be taken seriously. I was finally going to be the threat I knew I needed to be.

When Friday rolled around, I went to open gym and asked the guy, "Yo, did you bring it?"

"Aw, man," he said. "I forgot. I'll bring it next week."

Next week, same thing. Though everyone in the hood knows that guy that can get anything, we also know that guy is usually unreliable.

The thing is, the whole time I was waiting for him to bring me the gun, all I kept thinking was, *So this is where I am. I'm relying on this gun to protect me and my family, and it's not even real. Just like me. I'm a fraud.* I remember my father repeatedly telling me as I was growing up that the lowest a man could fall was when he needed a gun under his pillow to sleep. I was already dabbling in drugs, I'd become a womanizer, and my anger was out of control. Now, to top it all off, I needed a gun to feel human. These thoughts kept playing over and over in my mind until all I could think was, *I need help.* Or worse, *Maybe I should get a real gun and use it on myself.*

The next week in school, I ran into a dude named Jeremy Baker. Jeremy was a year older than me and was one of the few other Black males in the pilot program I was in. He was kind of quiet and kept to himself, but I had heard he was a really good rapper.

Now, I had done a little cafeteria battle rapping myself, and I had seen the movie *8 Mile*, so naturally, I thought I was a rapper. When I ran into Jeremy, I said, "Hey, man, I heard you were a rapper. You wanna battle sometime?"

He paused before answering, "I actually don't battle. I'm a Christian rapper."

I didn't even know where to go with that. I mean, if you had looked at my BlackPlanet page (Facebook for Black people before Facebook existed) under religion, you would have seen "Christian," but Christianity was just culture for me. I'd never thought about Jesus having so much influence on me that I'd need to reference Him for what I should or shouldn't do. That was all *my* choice. But Jeremy just threw it out there without any qualifications. No fear that I might think he was soft or lame. He was a Christian, and because of that, there were things he wouldn't do. He was unashamed.

"Oh, okay," I said. "Cool." And that was it.

A couple days later, Jeremy was outside eating lunch, and when I walked over, I noticed there was a CD on the table. It had a guy on the front with dreadlocks like mine going down his back, a red bandana across his forehead, another one across his mouth, and a long necklace with a key on the end of it. Then I saw the name of the album.

"Bloody Streets Volume One," I read aloud. Seeing my chance to remedy the cognitive dissonance he had caused, I said, "Yo, I thought you were a Christian. Why are you listening to this? This looks like murder music."

"No, man," he said, calmly shaking his head. "This is Christian music."

I was not convinced. "Fam, it's called 'Bloody Streets.' This man is clearly about to rob a bank. How is this Christian music?"

He just smiled at me. "Take it home. Listen to it."

I picked it up. It had one of those parental advisory stickers on it, but on closer inspection, the sticker actually said, "This album is not to be sold. It is only to be given away for free." I had never seen that before.

"Go ahead," Jeremy said again. "Take it. See what you think."

So I did. The project had eight songs on it. I loved every single one. The first seven weaved a compelling story of the rapper's life. His stage name had previously been Synista, and he was the front man of a group that was making a lot of noise in Tampa and getting the attention of some major labels. Like many rappers, he was involved in a lot of street activity—drug dealing, shoot-outs, and wild escapades. But at the height of all that, he experienced this dark moment that he described as coming face-to-face with the devil. He deduced from that experience, "If the devil is real, God must be real." He bolted to his grandmother's house, where she instructed him to read through the Psalms. When he read Psalm 23—the one that begins "The Lord is my shepherd"—God began to change him radically. He left his old life behind, dropped the *S* from his name, and became Mynista. The eighth song on the album was a gospel presentation.

After listening to his story, I believed the gospel Mynista sang about. And that day, at my own grandmother's house, I believed on Christ as my Lord and Savior, and I've literally been walking with Jesus ever since.

I never did get that gun. I told my friend I didn't want it anymore. Jesus had restored my security. As I learned of His promises and His commitments to me and my flourishing, they became infinitely more protective than extended clips and six-inch blades. I learned who God was and almost immediately saw who I was supposed to be. Jesus gave me an invincibility not based on *my* ability to defeat others in conflict but in *His* defeat of death, sin, and the devil—the ultimate source of conflict in my soul. I saw that the hood didn't belong to whatever gang was claiming authority. It belonged to God. In a song I later wrote called "Crowns and Thorns," I said, "I've never been a place that my God don't reign."[1] In other words, I have never stepped foot onto a square inch of this planet that didn't fall under God's jurisdiction. Nobody can touch me unless God allows it, and if He does allow it, He still has me! Whoever threatens the sons and daughters of God is always in far more danger, because God is with His children.

All my life I had wanted to be dangerous. Someone who is not to be played with. Someone whose presence demands respect, admiration, even fear, simply because of who he is. Resources, power, and respect are hip-hop's holy trinity. To have these is to achieve a kind of god status. The man or woman that commands this triune reality is truly the dangerous one.

But what I saw in the face of Jesus is the quintessence of all we've longed for—more resources, more power, and so worthy of respect that every knee will bow and every tongue will confess that He is truly "that guy."

I am reminded of the iconic scene from the hit series *Breaking Bad* where Walter White is explaining to his wife the power of his drug operation and why she should not fear that his enemies might hurt their family. Walter says the threats that his enemies pose to him pale in comparison to the threat that he is to his enemies. He says, "I am not in danger; I am the danger."

Jesus most certainly kept the same kind of energy in my life. All of the strongholds that plagued my existence were overpowered by the stronger hold of the Lord Jesus Christ. Everything must adjust to Him. He puts danger in danger.

He is the most dangerous man that ever lived.

CHAPTER 1

DANGEROUS JESUS

Many men claimed Him but did He ever claim them?
"NEW PORTRAIT"

No one was more dangerous than the Lord Jesus.

From the moment He arrived on the scene, Jesus posed a threat to the unjust, a threat to the oppressors, and a threat to every semblance of authority wielded by the kingdom of darkness.

Jesus' life is what happens when all that is good, true, and beautiful is perfectly embodied in a human being living in a world that is the opposite of all three—so much so that His very existence became an act of rebellion.

He invaded the world with love for the forgotten, hope for the hopeless, and freedom for the bound. His theme song of mercy, grace, and truth defied anyone and anything that dared to play a different tune.

His ideas were disruptive, subversive, and dare I say scandalous to the world around Him. They challenged the status quo and turned the ancient world upside down.

Who else would choose the ghetto of Nazareth over the palaces of Egypt as His home, not just in time but forever? The man who claims to reign for all eternity will forever be called Jesus *of Nazareth*, that is, Jesus of the ghetto. The place "nothing good comes from" becomes the place that everything good depends on!

Who else would entrust his gospel message to a group of disciples who were thought of as uneducated and lacking in speaking skills? I love the moment at Pentecost when the Holy Spirit gives Jesus' disciples the ability to speak in other languages. The onlooking crowd is amazed because these disciples from Galilee were known to use improper, barbaric speech. It's equivalent to the way some people today prejudicially look down on Ebonics. But Jesus, the Word made flesh, entrusted His gospel to the dialect of the poor.

Who else would form a movement not from kings or high priests but from the needy and the forgotten?

Who else would define greatness as humility and service, not riches and excess?

Who else would teach that the best thing for me centers around intentionally thinking about what's best for my neighbor—even when my neighbor doesn't deserve it?

Who else preached loving your enemy, forgiving your offender, and giving to those who can do nothing for you in return?

Who else would structure their kingdom on the first coming last and weakness being an advantage? The very people the world calls supremely weak—the poor, the meek, the peacemakers—He calls supremely blessed. The world steps over the least of these in the society. Jesus says, "I *am* the least of these. An assault on them is an assault on me."

In an otherwise barbaric culture, Jesus advocated nonviolence. He told people, "If anyone slaps you on your right cheek, turn the other to him also."[1]

Jesus redefined love and radically shifted our understanding of what it means to be a lover of people. John 3:16, perhaps the best-known verse in the Bible, says, "God so loved the world, that he gave his only Son, that whoever believes in him should not perish but have eternal life" (ESV). That's it right there. That's the shift. Love is demonstrated not by what we hold on to but by what we are willing to give up.

But this Jesus was more than just a godly man with good ideas. This Jesus was God in the flesh, who secured every promise He made with divine certainty. This Jesus' life, death, and glorious resurrection is not just the point of *His* story; it is indeed the point of *history*. Everything that Jesus accomplishes He claims as a win that extends to the entire cosmos.

This Jesus started His ministry by turning water into wine, and He ended His ministry by raising a man from the dead. In doing so, this Jesus demonstrates—both by festival and by funeral—that redemption will always have the final word.

This Jesus' birth, life, death, and resurrection pattern the course of history. Things live, things suffer, but—blessed be our God—things will have their redemption. It's a genius flex. What other savior can say that the redemption of an imperfect world will be more glorious than a perfect world that never needed redemption?

Jesus was so dangerous, the powers that be killed Him. But the joke is always on the opposition—this Jesus can't be canceled. Three days later, when He rose from the dead, He became even *more* dangerous, because His life is nothing short of contagious.

Even today, Jesus poses a threat to the status quo. He's a threat to our division. He's a threat to our rebellion. But the beautiful thing is, He's a good threat. I mean, if I got termites in my house, I want someone to bring the poison, you know what I mean?

To the degree that someone holds power, they can become a threat for unimaginable good or a threat for unimaginable harm. Take Rachael Denhollander.

THREAT TO THE THREAT

Rachael Denhollander was a young gymnast from Kalamazoo, Michigan. When she was fifteen, she was sexually abused by Dr. Larry Nassar—and she was not alone. Nassar was the team doctor for USA Gymnastics, and over the course of two decades, he sexually abused hundreds of young girls. The long-term emotional damage he caused was unimaginable. One of the girls he abused even committed suicide. And because he was so powerful, the girls he hurt were afraid to speak out against him. They were afraid that they wouldn't be believed. That they would get in trouble. That their own reputations would be damaged. So he just kept on going, kept on hurting.

Other people in positions of power—members of law enforcement, officials at the university where he worked, the powers that be at USA Gymnastics—could have stopped him. They were told what was happening. But they didn't do anything. And their lack of willingness to use their power for good made Nassar even more powerful.

That's the thing about power. In the wrong hands, left unchecked, it can do unspeakable damage, like a tornado or a hurricane. But in the right hands, power can also do unimaginable good.

Enter Rachael Denhollander. Rachael, animated by her relentless trust in the Lord Jesus Christ, stood up to Larry Nassar. She shared her story. She got others to listen. She raised up an army of fellow survivors, and together, they took Nassar down.

Larry Nassar was dangerous. But Rachael Denhollander was even more dangerous. She became a terror to terror.

Nobody was, is, or will be a greater threat to evil than Jesus. He is the kind of dangerous that is so infused with power from on high that nothing stays the same when He walks into the room. His love is so strong, it's intoxicating. His truth is so good, it sets people free. And His peace is so resilient, it doesn't make natural sense—it "surpasses all understanding."[2] This is the scary good Savior, Jesus the Christ.

Here we sit, two thousand years after Jesus lived, died, and was resurrected, and Jesus is the most admired figure in history, boasting a following in the billions. But the paradox of this Jesus is that even though He is the most observed man in history, He is simultaneously the most ignored. And perhaps worse than ignored, He is the

THE ONLY THING MORE DANGEROUS THAN GETTING JESUS RIGHT IS GETTING JESUS WRONG.

most weaponized, reinterpreted, and misappropriated figure in history. And the only thing more dangerous than getting Jesus right is getting Jesus wrong.

A GOOD KIND OF CONTAGIOUS

Jesus, understood correctly, spawns life. From Martin Luther to Martin Luther King, from Lemuel Haynes to Dietrich Bonhoeffer, Jesus produces world-changing, life-sacrificing, heaven-summoning, dangerous Christians. This is precisely what we see in the early years of the church.

Rodney Stark, a sociologist of religion, studied the rise of Christianity in an effort to make sense of how, with no weapons, no wealth, and no position of influence in society, within just three centuries, Jesus' followers grew from twelve disciples into millions of followers across the globe. My good friend Keas Keasler boils down the following points:[3]

First, there was a "radical reordering of social relations." In other words, people from different ethnic and social groups treated each other as family.

Then, "women were given higher status" and were allowed to lead in worship. Up to that point, all pagan religions were dominated by men.

The early Christians "practiced radical hospitality toward one another and toward outsiders." They saw strangers as neighbors and neighbors as family.

They refused to use violence to spread their movement. The early church "was completely nonviolent," and "for its first three hundred years of existence," Christians did not see partnership with the state as the means to spread Christianity.

They "showed compassionate care for the poor and stayed in cities during plagues to care for the sick." In the days of the early church, the Plague of Galen "devastated the known world." Because there was no way to stop it, when the plague arrived in a city, everyone left the sick to fend for themselves. But "historians note there was one group that stayed behind to care for the sick": Christians. And many died as a result.

They "willingly went to martyrdom while praying for their captors." They weren't afraid of death, and even showed love to those who killed them.

They "took in unwanted babies." Roman law allowed people to abandon unwanted newborns outside of the city, leaving them to be killed in the outlying areas by weather or wild animals. But Christians not only refused to engage in this practice; they would also rescue babies who had been abandoned because they believed each one was "created in the image of God and someone whom Christ had died for."

One of the most profound observations that came out of Stark's research, though, is that it was not what the believers *taught* (important as it was) that made them so impressive to the outside world; it was how they *lived out* what they said they believed. They followed in the footsteps of the good-dangerous Jesus.

This brings us to, as I see it, the biggest problem for American Christianity today—we've too often separated Jesus' words from His walk. Dallas Willard used the term "vampire Christians" to describe those who say to Jesus, in essence, "I'd like a little of your blood, please. But I don't care to be your student or have your character. In fact, won't you just excuse me while I get on with my life, and I'll see you in heaven."[4]

The blood of Jesus and what it affords us—eternal life and

It is of little benefit to have the words of Jesus in our mouths and not the ways of Jesus on our feet.

forgiveness of sin—are the essential perks of the package. But we try to bifurcate the perks of His blood from the person who shed that blood. In other words, we want what He can do for us, but we don't want to engage with what we are called to do through Him. It is of little benefit to have the words of Jesus in our mouths and not the ways of Jesus on our feet.

This is precisely why so many of us think spirituality is merely doing our devotions every morning—just us and God. Devotions are important, but true religion—the religion God is pleased with—is demonstrated in action. Christianity is doing what Jesus did. He lived among us, loving, healing, and caring for others, along with teaching about His Kingdom.

The Christian faith, as exemplified by the early church, is the most complete, life-altering, world-changing, supernatural, God-blessed institution on this planet. Like yeast in dough, it permeates all of society. It transforms cultures. It brings the dead to life. It is literally connected to the risen Savior. It's an unstoppable, immovable force. But when the Christian faith moves from the pure Christianity of Christ to what the great emancipator Frederick Douglass referred to as the Christianity of the Land—"where the church regards religion simply as a form of worship, an empty ceremony. . . . A worship that can be conducted by persons who refuse to give shelter to the homeless, to give bread to the hungry, [and] clothing to the naked"—it becomes "a curse, not a blessing to mankind."[5] The Christianity of Christ, like Jesus Himself, is dangerous to the forces of evil. The Christianity of the Land is often a participant in that very evil.

THE CHRISTIANITY OF THE LAND

There has been no body of work that's influenced my faith like what I have termed "slave theology"—the witness of enslaved Africans in the antebellum South. During this time, people on plantations all over the country made every attempt possible to destroy, thwart, and pervert slaves' interest in Jesus—from attacking my ancestors' ability to read to, when that didn't work, creating slave Bibles that omitted all the verses about freedom to routinely sending white and commissioned Black preachers to tell my ancestors that their destiny was bondage because of their subhuman status. I have a theology work from the slave era titled *"The Negro a Beast," or "In the Image of God."* The conclusion of the slave-owning author is the former. In fact, almost 50 percent of all literature defending American slavery was written by Bible-believing Christians.[6]

That may be why Charles Spurgeon once said, "It is the Church of Christ that keeps his brethren under bondage; if it were not for that Church, the system of slavery would go back to the hell from which it sprung."[7]

Perhaps most damning, however, was the general fear that enslaved Africans had of their masters who claimed to be Christians. In fact, slaves would pray that their masters were *not* religious because religious masters were usually worse. Fredrick Douglass said he remembers watching his master, Thomas Auld, beat a fellow slave to an inch of his life, gather himself, and then go inside for family devotions.

Yet Jesus, through some kind of divine intervention, was still able to have a profound impact on the people who were being abused in His name. Slaves formed their own churches in defiance. Negro spirituals served as testaments of hope and resilience. And to this day, African Americans are statistically more likely to follow Jesus than the general population. They're more likely to read their Bibles. They're more likely to attend church and pray regularly. And they're more likely to say that the Bible and Jesus are central to their life.[8]

This is not the result of brainwashing. Brainwashing typically reproduces the indoctrination and behavior of the oppressor in its victims, yet these men and women denounced the faith of their enslavers. In defiance of what they were taught, the slave church believed the Bible was their path to freedom and that Jesus was on the side of the oppressed. They simply understood, theologically, who Jesus was: Jesus was an ethnic minority who was marginalized by the religious establishment and executed by the state.

In fact, there is nothing from theologian Jonathan Edwards (who, by the way, was able to write theology for thirteen hours a day because he had slaves taking care of his property) or the Great Awakening that impresses me like what God was doing in the hearts of slaves in the midst of a mainstream misrepresentation of who He actually was.

Douglass framed the conundrum like this:

> I love the pure, peaceable, and impartial Christianity of Christ:
> I therefore hate the corrupt, slaveholding, women-whipping,
> cradle-plundering, partial and hypocritical Christianity of this
> land. Indeed, I can see no reason, but the most deceitful one,
> for calling the religion of this land Christianity. I look upon it
> as the climax of all misnomers, the boldest of all frauds, and
> the grossest of all libels.[9]

Brothers and sisters, I contend that the boldest of all frauds is a Christianity born of human imagination parading around as the Christianity of Christ, and the battle of the ages is separating the pure Christianity of Christ from the corrupt Christianity of the Land. Because the Christianity of the Land is not Christian at all. We must all take a hard look in the mirror and ask ourselves: *Which Christianity am I proclaiming?*

REAL AND PRESENT DANGER

Over the past several years, I have watched a surge of people I love walk away from Jesus, disillusioned by the church. And that is not just anecdotal. Studies show that for every person who enters the Christian faith, four leave.[10] And from what I have observed, few have cited Marxism, critical race theory, or secularism as the culprit. It was not the world that pulled them away from Jesus. It was people claiming to belong to the church. Almost all the individuals I know that have had their faith shipwrecked have cited the politicizing of Christianity and their church's apathy—and often hostility—toward justice and other issues concerning neighborly love.

The problem is that what is often propagated as mainstream Christianity is simply not worthy of the name. It is an updated Christianity of the Land. People have believed in a version of Jesus that is either silent or complicit in enabling what is clearly wrong.

Now, when I refer to the politicizing of Christianity, I have a word for my brothers and sisters on the political right before we go any further. I suspect throughout this book, some people who find themselves in this space may feel I am being one-sided in my critique of the Christianity of the Land. But the reason why my critique may seem more strongly aimed at the right is because most often, the political left is not concerned about representing Jesus. Rather, it is the conservative side—admittedly, the side of the aisle I lean—that is often referencing Jesus as a sponsor of their politics. And if they're claiming my Lord, then I'm inevitably going to have more to say to them concerning how they may (mis)represent Him. It was the same with Jesus in the Gospels—remember, there were a lot of religious alternatives in Jesus' day, but He zoned in on the Pharisees in part because they were the ones who considered themselves representatives of His Father. So when I write about the Christianity of the Land and its intersections with partisan politics, I do so as a lover of the reputation of Jesus and as somewhat of an affiliate of the tribe.

More than two thousand years ago, Jesus asked His disciples, "Who do people say that the Son of Man is?" and His disciples responded, "Some say John the Baptist; others, Elijah; still others Jeremiah or one of the prophets." But then Jesus directed the question squarely at them: "Who do *you* say that I am?" And Peter responded, "You are the Messiah, the Son of the living God."[11]

Let's walk that same question out today. There are many prominent representations of Jesus. But who do *we* think He is?

Is He ultra-right-wing Jesus, who spins a Christianity that is hostile toward the vulnerable and defensive of the powerful?

Is He condemnation Jesus, who spins a Christianity that insists people know they are wrong without insisting they know they are loved?

Is He patriot Jesus, who spins a Christianity that places America at the center of the universe, making the success of the United States tantamount to the success of God Himself?

Is He weak Jesus, who spins a Christianity steeped in fear and fragility, consumed with threat-finding and a subsequent retreat from culture?

Is He "vibes" Jesus, who spins a Christianity that is partner to our good time but never challenges us to be righteous?

Is He winning Jesus, who spins a Christianity that associates the presence of God with success with little to say about suffering?

Is He overspiritual Jesus, who spins a Christianity that scoffs at therapy, science, and any kind of pleasure perceived as worldly?

> **JESUS IS NOT WHO WE *WANT* HIM TO BE. HE IS WHO HE IS AND ALWAYS HAS BEEN.**

If we are following the real Jesus, the answer is "none of the above." Jesus is not who we *want* Him to be. He is who He is and always has been. *He* didn't change. We did. We have too often perverted true Christianity into a Christianity of the Land, a Christianity devoid of Christ. And a Christianity that is devoid of Christ is a danger to all that is good.

There must be a recasting and a revival of what it means to truly belong to Jesus—the *real* Jesus. The Messiah. The Son of the living God. Likewise, there must be a recasting and a revival of true Christianity. We need to reclaim Christianity from the land and restore it to the pure, peaceable Christianity of the risen Christ.

A Christianity that cares for the marginalized, the poor, and the oppressed.

A Christianity with a global Savior and a global agenda that is influenced by what God is doing all over the world, not simply in suburban America.

A Christianity that is as not *of* this world as it is *in* this world, meaning it has an actual effect on people's spiritual, social, economic, and environmental state.

A Christianity whose adherents are bringing the culture of heaven down to the culture of earth.

A Christianity that does not pit a biblical sexual ethic against genuinely caring for those whose lifestyles it doesn't endorse. A Christianity that loves marriage and a biblical sexual ethic as much as it loves those who oppose it.

An enemy-loving, humility-pursuing, and others-centering Christianity is indeed the Christianity of Christ. That Christianity is a good kind of dangerous. That kind of Christianity is a threat to evil—a terror to terror. That Christianity changes the world. That peaceable, pure, good-dangerous Christianity of Christ is exactly the Christianity the world is thirsty for!

If people reject our Savior, let it be because they reject Him for *Him*, not because they are repelled by a caricature of Him—a being of our own creation that only borrows His name.

Brothers and sisters, we need a revival. Better said, we need a recovery, because it's not a new Jesus we're talking about but a true Jesus.

We need to reconnect with the real Jesus—the most dangerous man I know.

We need to follow in the footsteps of this dangerous Jesus. We need to again become a threat to the threats.

Let the pure and peaceable Christianity of Christ rise, making the church dangerous for good once again.

CHAPTER 2

DANGEROUS FAITH

Who's in more danger, the persecuted or the comfortable?
"CROWNS & THORNS (OCEANS)"

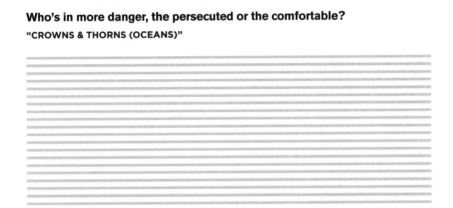

It felt like I was staring down the barrel of a loaded shotgun.

So, KB . . . The voice echoed in my head. *Is this Jesus stuff actually real to you?*

At that moment, imagining those two dark holes drawing down at me, I wasn't sure.

The question came at me again, this time with more intensity than I was ready for: *Are you ready to lay down your life for Jesus?*

I turned slightly to my left and took a quick visual inventory of the other six people in the room. It was clear I wasn't the only person shaken to the core over what we had just witnessed. We had gathered at my pastor's house to watch a documentary on a particular area in West Africa that our church was sponsoring a mission trip to, and now that it was over, we all had some serious soul searching to do.

Just forty-five minutes earlier, I had sauntered into the room, bubbling with excitement, anticipation, and confidence. This wasn't my first rodeo. My bachelor of arts is in missions with an emphasis on foreign mission. I had already served in eight countries in Africa the previous year, so I figured this would be a breeze. I thought, *We'll kiss some babies, take a few selfies for Instagram, and I'll be home by the end of the month to judge everyone in America for being so privileged and ungrateful.*

But all that excitement and swagger evaporated like water on hot pavement as the film revealed the full extent of what we were walking into—the civil war, the child soldiers, the mass sexual assaults on the country's women, the sadistic cannibalism, the government corruption, and—as if that wasn't enough—the rampant witchcraft.

We all sat in stunned silence after watching in horror as depravity danced in front of us in 3D. The warning *You might actually die* ricocheted through my head so loudly, I was surprised the others couldn't hear it too.

Now our pastor stood before us—all of us hollowed-out shells of the people we had been when the evening began. He gently affirmed the goodness of our desire for physical safety. He assured us that no one should feel guilty about wanting to preserve the life God has given us and that no one would be judged if they decided to drop out of the trip.

Given the vibe of the room, I half expected him to close with a reassuring, "It's really not as bad as it looks." The tension would break, we'd all smile and laugh, and then we'd say a quick group prayer and be on our way.

Instead, he looked each of us in the eye, and with gravity in his voice, he said, "To go on this trip is to lay your life down for Jesus. Full stop. But if we lose our lives in pursuit of God's call, it will be worth it."

I was speechless, which felt purposeful, because it's in my inability to speak that God often speaks the loudest.

The voice echoed through my head again. *Is this Jesus stuff actually real to you?*

I mean, I knew God had my back. But sitting there in that living room, a lukewarm bottle of water in my hand, it was as if God Himself had posed the question, *If you don't trust Me to be your God in West Africa, how can you trust Me to be your God anywhere?*

Touché, God. Touché.

I wrestled hard on my drive home. I thought, *I'm only twenty-four years old. I've only been married for two years. I want to start a family. I have albums I want to record, books I want to write, dreams and purposes I've yet to fulfill.*

I've got to get out of this, I thought, and I felt perfectly justified in finding an excuse. I just needed a good one.

Michelle.

Yeah, that would do it. I was going to use my lovely wife as a get-out-of-jail-free card. I'd just go to my pastor and be like, "Hey, I'm down. I mean, you know me. I'm Martin Luther Kingdom, Mr. Jesus-over-Everything. I'm ready to go, but the wife, yeah . . . she's not okay with it. You know how it is." And I'd be home free without losing face.

When I got home, I held up at the door for a minute. This was going to take some work. I had to come across as confident and self-assured but not so much that Michelle would think, *Yeah, babe, you got this.* I decided to take the pastor's approach—just put it out there and let the reality hit her hard, the way it hit me. I took a deep breath, opened the door, and zeroed right in on Michelle, who was standing at the far end of the living room.

"Babe," I said, reaching over and grabbing her hand, "I need to talk to you right now. It's serious."

"What is it?" She had a concerned look on her face. *Perfect.*

I pulled her over to the couch. "I think you need to have a seat," I said. "This is not something you are gonna want to hear."

"Why, what happened?"

A soon as we sat down, I was like, "Listen. I know we talked about me doing this mission trip, and I was all excited about it. And I'm still excited about it." *There you go.* "But this trip is not your typical mission trip. There's some bad stuff going on in this place, babe, and I mean *really* bad, like people shooting at each other, cannibalism, witchcraft. And we're going to be going into the jungle. Pastor says a missionary even got killed there not too long ago." She just stared at me intently. This was it. This was my chance.

"I mean . . . one member of the team is making a goodbye video for his mom, in case he doesn't return." I paused for a second to let the thought of a KB-less existence sink in. "Now, you know me," I assured her. "I'm totally cool with that. But the thing is, this isn't just about me. I need to know *you're* okay with it."

She hadn't even blinked. There was no doubt in my mind that the next words out of her mouth were going to be, "Of course you can't go. I need you to be here." I glanced at the clock. Pastor was probably still awake. I could still call him tonight, and this whole thing would be over and done with. Then Michelle gripped my hand tighter and said, "Is God calling you to do this trip?"

"What?"

"Do you feel like God is calling you to go on this trip?"

I heard her. I just couldn't figure out her angle.

"Well . . . I guess so . . . yeah."

"Okay, then," she said. "I think you should go."

Wait a minute . . .

I let go of her hand and sat back, a little offended. "Hold up, baby," I said. "You trying to get rid of me or something? I mean, we've only been married for a few years. Don't you want this to go longer?" She just stared at me somberly. I gave it one last go. "I mean . . . what if I don't come back?"

Without skipping a beat, my beautiful, amazing, loving wife looked me square in the eye and said, "If you don't come back, God will take care of me."

For the second time that night, I was shook—this time, not by fear, but by the faith of my wife. She was keyed in to a profound truth. Our lives don't belong to us. They belong to the One who gave them to us. How we felt personally about the situation wasn't of first importance. It wasn't about what I wanted or what she wanted. It was about discerning what *He* wanted.

When Jesus was crying out to God in the garden of Gethsemane, His disciples had all fallen asleep, Judas had sold Him out, the guards were on their way, and knowing full well what was coming for Him, Jesus "fell facedown and prayed, 'My Father, if it is possible, let this cup pass from me. Yet not as I will, but as you will.'"[1] Jesus, whose will was always good, still preferred His Father's will over His own.

When I think about the words of Jesus in the context of my own will, I am convinced that only a fool would prefer his limited, corrupted, unreliable, often wrong will over the perfect, divine, faithful will of the living God. I was forced to remind myself of the superiority of following the call of God over the call of self-preservation. Eternity will prove that nobody has ever trusted God and been truly disappointed. Unlike my will, God's will can be trusted. God has me.

I spent a lot of time that night in prayer. Here I was, performing on all these stages and telling people that Jesus is better than life and that "to live is Christ and to die is gain," but now it was go time, and I wasn't so sure anymore. I continued to be faced with hard questions like, *If Jesus is as good as you make Him seem in your music—if He is as worthy as you make Him seem—if that God is your God in Tampa, will He not be in West Africa?* I mean, it's a fair request to ask for God's protection, guidance, and presence in my life if I were to go to West Africa, because that's a hard place to serve. But didn't I need the same level of protection and guidance here? In all the places where I'd served God, it was the hard places where it was easiest to trust Him and the easy places where it was hardest.

Cowardice always elevates self at the expense of trusting God. And self is always less rewarding.

Those questions eventually led me to the conclusion that really, the harder place to love God is right here in the United States, because here we rarely feel tested to *prove* that we actually love Him. Going to West Africa, however, would give me an opportunity to test the validity of my assumption—to put myself in a position where God could flex the brilliance of His promise to be with me to the ends of the earth.

THERE IS NO WAY TO KNOW THAT GOD IS BETTER THAN LIFE WHILE SIMULTANEOUSLY HOLDING ON TO LIFE LIKE IT IS BETTER THAN GOD.

I ended up going on that trip, not because my fear had dissipated, but because it became clear to me that there is no way to know that God is better than life while simultaneously holding on to life like it is better than God. It's like Charles Spurgeon said: "If Christ be anything He must be everything."[2]

That trip became the blueprint for how I longed to live my life everywhere. There's nowhere on this planet—whether I'm at the Ritz-Carlton or on the south side of St. Pete—where my need for God changes. It doesn't necessarily increase or decrease depending on where I'm at. But if such a thing were the case, my need for God would most certainly *increase* where I feel most comfortable and safe. It is there that I tend to forget Him. That's when spiritual atrophy kicks in—when our circumstances tempt us to believe that we can handle things ourselves.

No doubt, going to West Africa was dangerous. But, brothers and sisters, what is more dangerous is not being faithful to the bidding of our God. Our faith is more at risk—is *most* at risk—when it is cultivated without risk. I went to West Africa trusting that God would grant me the gift of safety, but safety is not my god.

"DO THIS OR YOU WILL DIE"

Gordon Ramsay, the world-famous chef, is probably one of my favorite celebrities. I know the man's tongue seems to be set on fire by the flames of hell, but because I find British accents polite, I have no problem looking past that to the results of his leadership and culinary genius. When I watch *Kitchen Nightmares*, one of Chef Ramsay's shows, I'm always astonished that people are resistant to his advice. The show follows Chef Ramsay as he arrives at a restaurant that is completely falling apart—ants, roaches, subpar equipment, terrible food—and tries to help the owners turn their restaurant around. Ramsay profiles the mess for the owners and tells them what they need to do, essentially saying, "Do these things or you will die." But despite Ramsay's expertise, the owners often hit back with, "But we've had this chef for years" or "But we've always done things this way" or "But this recipe was passed down from my great grandfather's second cousin's uncle in Tuscany."

Now, Chef Ramsay is one of the most successful chefs in the world. He owns thirty-five restaurants across ten countries and has been awarded sixteen Michelin stars, the Academy Awards of food. Dude knows what he is talking about! So as scary and extreme as his advice might seem, if he walked into your kitchen and said, "Do this or you will die," wouldn't you be a fool not to do what he said—to surrender to the man?

As much as I hate comparing Jesus to Gordon Ramsay, this is exactly the conundrum we find ourselves in. Jesus is always keen to point out that we don't want salvation; we want sedation. "Make me comfortable while I die." Jesus shows up with the power of who He is, assesses our lives, and says, "Do these things or you will die," and how do we typically respond? John 6 is a great example.

Jesus has gained the following of thousands of people. His disciples have watched Him perform miracles like healing people, feeding the masses with the equivalent of a Lunchable, and even walking on water! Jesus says to the people, "I am the bread of life. No one who comes to me will ever be hungry, and no one who believes in me will ever be thirsty again." This seems like something the people want, yet when He tells them there's just one caveat—I need to be Lord of your life—folks respond, "This teaching is hard. Who can accept it?"[3] Jesus, the Good Shepherd, says to the sheep, "I must become your ALL or I am nothing to you," and they're hitting back with, "Yeah . . . we just want the bread, not the baker." Jesus even ups the offer, saying, "If you follow me, not only will you not die, you will live an abundant life," and still, "many of his disciples turned back and no longer walked with him."[4]

More than two thousand years later, the question for us—no matter how scary it might seem—is still, will you surrender to Him?

Surrender is the lifeblood of the dangerous Christian's life. Throw caution to the wind! Tell the Lord, *Where You lead me, I will follow, because only You know where You are going. What You say, I will do. Only You have the words of eternal life.*

Think of the specs of the abundant life that Jesus offers:

- faith that moves mountains
- faith that transforms lives
- faith that overcomes death
- faith that is the point of existence
- faith that gives joy in suffering
- faith that sets free

The context in which any of these specs moves from "ideals explained" to "lived experience" is our willingness to follow Jesus into the scary places. And the scary places are not simply (or even primarily) mission trips but rather anywhere or anything that God calls you to that fear tries to talk you out of. It's resisting temptation, letting go of an offense, or perhaps ending an ungodly

Surrender is the lifeblood of the dangerous Christian's life.

relationship—following Him into that scary obedience. Because, brothers and sisters, there is a lot of comfort in cowardice, but the experience of God is in courage.

STAND UP

Richard Wurmbrand was a pastor in Romania in the 1940s, right around the time Communism was taking over there. Just before the government attacked the churches, Wurmbrand and a group of other pastors gathered together to formulate a response.

When they asked the question, "Who is going to resist the Communist regime?" nobody stood up. After a few uncomfortable moments, Wurmbrand's wife, Sabina, leaned over and basically said to him, "You need to stand up and wipe the shame off our Lord's face."

He turned back to his wife and was like, "You know if I stand up, you're going to be a widow, right?" To which she replied, "I'd rather be a widow than married to a coward."

So Richard Wurmbrand stood up and rebuked everyone in the room for not doing the same. Shortly thereafter, the Communist regime captured Wurmbrand and threw him in prison, where he spent the next three years in solitary confinement in a small, windowless, underground cell.

Undeterred, Wurmbrand held fast to his faith and spent his days and nights composing sermons and spreading the gospel to his fellow inmates by tapping out messages on his cell wall in Morse code.

He was arrested again years later and sentenced to an additional twenty-five years in jail, where he was brutally beaten and subject to unthinkable acts of torture. He wrote an amazing book called *Tortured for Christ*, and after emigrating to America, he and his wife (who also spent three years in prison) went on to establish The Voice of the Martyrs, an international ministry dedicated to advocating for the persecuted church all over the world.

I have always been inspired by Wurmbrand's story because it proves something I have believed for some time: faith is not demonstrated on platforms but in the trenches. Having endured years of unspeakable pain and suffering, Wurmbrand said he was able to meet with God in those jail cells in ways he could never describe and that not even the cell walls or the batons of the guards could break his nearness to God or the presence of God in his life.

This is why America, though rarely a place of Christian persecution, is such a hard place to be a Christian. The blessing of safety can easily be perverted into an occasion for not taking God seriously.

CLIMATE CONTROL

It's been said that in the United States, our faith is too "air-conditioned," meaning we have faith in Jesus as long as the climate where we exercise that faith stays cool and under control. It's too easy for us to talk God and not walk God because there are tons of opportunities for us to talk (Twitter, Facebook, Snapchat, conferences, and so on), and talking costs us nothing! But the currency of the Christianity of Christ is sacrifice.

Loving God and others is not demonstrated by parroting catchy slogans or retweeting a verse of the day. It is demonstrated by a willingness to be inconvenienced, to be made uncomfortable, and to adjust our own lives for the benefit of other people.

Nowhere is this principle better illustrated than in John 3:16, what I like to think of as the juice of all things considered love: "God so loved the world, that he gave his only Son, that whoever believes in him shall not perish but have eternal life" (ESV). Brothers and sisters, love is demonstrated not by what we hold on to—our possessions, our way of life—but by what we are willing to give up. And with each opportunity we are granted to give or let go of something in pursuit of God's call, we are made wealthier. We come alive!

Though convenience is not inherently bad, it is often love's biggest competitor. We build our muscles by working them past their limit, stretching and ripping them. It's painful, but without the ripping there is no growth; and without growth, there is no strength; and without strength, we become weak and ineffectual.

We've got a bunch of alligator parks here in Florida, and they're filled with massive, dinosaur-looking alligators. A lot of them are bright, almost fluorescent green, because they lie there for twenty-three hours a day doing nothing and moss just grows on their backs. They don't have to hunt for their food. A zookeeper tosses meat into the enclosure, and as a result, they balloon into these overweight prehistoric blobs. I mean, they could still hurt you if you got too close (so maybe it's good they are too fat to go after you), but if you let these massive animals loose in the wild, a much smaller predator could kill them in a heartbeat because the comforts of their environment have undone the full potential of their nature.

We don't really get the option to take it easy when it comes to faith. If we just sit back and get spoiled and docile and ineffective (which is exactly what the devil wants us to do), we will die. We must strengthen our faith daily through our willingness to sacrifice—especially for those around us. Our genuine willingness to lose for the sake of our neighbors' gain is the only way to maintain a healthy, thriving, dangerous faith and to live an abundant life.

MOVING FROM RHETORIC TO REALITY

It is easy to live a Christianity that leads not by example but by opinion. But this loose, fragile, shallow faith is often a thermometer for the outside culture, matching the temperature rather than being the thermostat that sets it. It's one thing to say we are Christ followers. It is another to *show* we are Christ followers—to authentically live it out. Examples are all over the place.

There seems to be no group of people more upset about the prospect of state-sanctioned gay marriage than evangelicals. Stopping the "gay agenda" by wielding the power of the state seems to be among the highest priorities of the evangelical movement. And yet a 2014 study from the Council on Contemporary Families shows that evangelicals are more likely to be divorced than the average American.[5] Are we more concerned with fighting for the sanctity of marriage in Washington than we are in our own homes?

Though I agree with the Bible's definition of marriage, what is the value in holding up signs at gay pride parades that say, "God Made Marriage Between a Man and a Woman," only to leave that parade and cheat on or divorce the spouse you are married to? Is that not profoundly half baked? Rhetoric protects marriage by fighting for its definitions. Reality protects marriage by reflecting the values of the Kingdom and actually loving your spouse.

Likewise, there are few issues where Christians place confidence in the state's ability to legislate righteousness more than the issue of abortion. Many of us are eager to protect life, particularly in its most vulnerable forms, but map the location of that protection to the polls every four years. In fact, for many evangelicals, this issue is the determining factor of their vote in every presidential election—regardless of how morally bankrupt a candidate may be. If a candidate stands on the right side of the pro-life debate, they can typically bank on significant religious support in absolute earnest.

My favorite conservative thinker, David French, was accused of having the blood of unborn babies on his hands if he did not vote for a pro-life presidential candidate. He responded with a list of rather shocking facts about the pro-life movement that sharply demonstrate the peril of putting rhetoric over reality. He argued that historically, "Presidents have been [almost] irrelevant to the abortion rate" and that, until 2017, the rates of abortion had declined under every president since 1990 (note that abortion saw its steepest decline under a pro-choice president and abortions actually increased from 2017 through 2020 under a pro-life president).[6]

Yet I recognize that as I write this, the Supreme Court, in a landmark decision, has overturned *Roe v. Wade,* sending the issue back to the states. And the temptation for many is to understand abortion so neatly that a pro-life Supreme Court victory can feel like a panacea, the end of a decades-long fight. But the reality is far more complicated than the rhetoric. The data unequivocally suggest that "abortion was more common when it was mostly illegal." Fewer women got abortions in 2017, when abortions were federally supported, than they did when abortion was banned. The reality runs deeper than political positions can account for. Gratitude is an appropriate reaction for what the Supreme Court has decided, but as D-French reminds us, let's look at this "not as the beginning of the end of abortion in the United States, but rather as the end of the beginning of a long struggle to remake our nation into a culture that is far more hospitable to mother and child." He writes,

> The simple truth is that if the pro-life movement wants to end abortion, it has to do much more work than merely banning abortion. . . .
>
> This . . . doesn't mean that pro-life Americans should cease working to provide legal protections for unborn life. As a matter of deep principle, we cannot leave any human being unprotected by law—and the life and health of the mother are as paramount as those of the child. But the historical record does tell us that ending abortion is a different matter from banning abortion, and we cannot end abortion until we learn why women seek abortions and how our nation can address the concerns that lead them to make that choice.[7]

French reminds us, "We're most passionate about the president. Yet too many of us are less interested in the crisis pregnancy center down the street. Without forsaking national politics, we can reverse that intensity, and if we reverse that intensity through loving, intentional outreach, we will reinforce the very decision the data and our experience tells us a woman wants to make."[8] David's point here is important: Politics are not irrelevant, but they are also not more powerful than the reality we create through our Christian witness.

Many abortions are motivated by single moms' fears that they will not be able to sufficiently provide for the child. Laws aside, how do we continue to incentivize life by creating a culture that welcomes, sustains, and helps mothers flourish? Studies show that many women who seek to terminate their babies do so as a last resort, and historically that last resort has not become less attractive by law and condemnation but by grace and empowerment. Because often in the context of the church, the fear of provision is compounded with the fear of being shamed. While virtually every church would tell those single mothers that abortion is wrong, how often are churches willing to throw a baby shower for a young, unwed mother-to-be? We all agree that a baby is a gift from God, and therefore we want single mothers to safely bring their babies into this world out of their duty to God. Yet our actions often don't communicate that those babies born out of wedlock are as valuable to God as those born in wedlock. We don't celebrate them as we should. We don't congratulate the unwed mother on bringing new life into the world. If we genuinely cherished new life, we would rally around the unwed mother, love her, and help her take care of the new life that we claim to value and fight to protect.

The salient reality is that we often don't know how to say that sex outside of marriage is a sin while at the same time honoring what that sex might produce. New life is to be praised, protected, and provided for—and that includes our *active* participation. But too often we prioritize the rhetoric of premarital abstinence over the reality of loving and caring for our unwed neighbors. Legislation is but a single way to protect life in the womb. And given that fewer abortions happen today than they did the year before *Roe v. Wade*,[9] legislation is not always the most effective way. But grace-driven love for both women and their babies, regardless of the context, creates a culture of life that abortion cannot survive.

I have also found that many churches are happy to engage in the conversation on racial reconciliation and justice for all—until it starts to affect their bottom line. I've heard story after story of pastors who have lost their jobs over even the slightest attempt to talk about racial injustice from the pulpit because certain members (who happened to be big donors) got upset and threatened to leave. In fact, a friend of ours who was doing a youth Bible study on Ephesians and made a passing comment about the need for racial reconciliation was fired almost immediately. The church even asked him to sign a nondisclosure agreement, whereby they agreed to keep him on salary until he transitioned into a new job as long as he didn't tell anyone why he was let go.

It may very well be that we're willing to talk about racial injustice and the need for reconciliation until we're confronted with the fact that those who resist racial progress are often stakeholders in our livelihood. I remember an incident where a gentleman working for a Christian organization said something very racist to a team member of mine. When this was brought to the attention of the owner of the organization, he responded, "I don't pay him not to be racist; I pay him to do his job." In other words, racists still pay bills, and confrontation is costly. I've seen firsthand sincere enthusiasm from pastors eager to make their church community more like heaven by tackling the racial issues that divide us, only to be met by the strongest resistance they've ever witnessed in the life of their ministry. But if there's one thing Jesus illustrates for us powerfully, it's that reconciliation ain't cheap. It cost Him His life.

Taking the rhetoric of racialization one step further, while most churches claim that they want diversity, the reality is much more suggestion than substance. Sociologist Michael Emerson conducted a study that found that "'all the growth [in multiracial churches] has been people of color moving into white churches,' and 'we have seen zero change in the percentage of whites moving into churches of color.' Once a multiracial church becomes less than 50% white . . . the white members leave."[10]

Emerson contends that "if Christians of different racial backgrounds began worshipping together, . . . racial reconciliation could follow."[11] I believe he is right. The problem is that creating a genuine multiracial church takes work and involves risk. It's not simply a question of welcoming people of color in but allowing God to transform our fellowship into something it's never been before. It means rethinking "who is up on the platform during worship and who is put into leadership and the ministry." It means rethinking "the artwork and the books you're using and the music you're playing. Does it reflect all people or only one culture?"[12] And given the findings of Emerson's study, it means being willing to risk losing certain members and possibly sacrificing your bottom line not just for the sake of diversity but also for the glory of God's multiracial bride—the church.

Korie L. Edwards, author of the book *The Elusive Dream: The Power of Race in Interracial Churches*, says, "I would argue that the goal shouldn't be diversity. Rather, all churches are called to be places of justice, uplifting the oppressed. . . . All churches, regardless of their racial and ethnic composition, should be like that. And then you can move toward integration."[13]

Amen to that. Rhetoric is cheap. Reality is costly. But the payoff from the latter utterly eclipses the former.

FIRE-TESTED FAITH

One of the biggest flaws of the Christianity of the Land is that it strives to be the default, the norm, so that it does not have to defend, explain itself to, or persuade anybody. It just *is*. And when the Christianity of the Land is not able to achieve its dominance through the persuasion lifestyle or a movement of God, the only option is to legislate it so it will essentially be illegal to behave otherwise.

The true Christianity of Christ, however, moves forward not by the strength of politics or fear or coercion but by the strength of a person, the Lord Jesus Christ. As important as security is, security is not God. God is our security. As Christ followers, we don't look to Washington or to a political party for our protection. We look to God Himself! He alone is "[our] refuge and [our] fortress, [our] God in whom [we] trust. . . . His faithfulness will be a protective shield."[14]

> **AS CHRIST FOLLOWERS, WE DON'T LOOK TO WASHINGTON OR TO A POLITICAL PARTY FOR OUR PROTECTION. WE LOOK TO GOD HIMSELF!**

Even more ludicrous than trusting in human institutions for protection is the notion that God Himself needs our protection. I've watched politician after politician dangle in front of the church the prospect of "protecting God" if they get elected. Politicians telling us they are going to "protect God" is a blasphemous thought!

Not only does God not need anybody's protection, nobody in Washington can protect my right to love Jesus. They didn't grant me that right, so I am never in "danger" of them taking it away. I am free to love and worship Jesus even if the government comes after me. Much love and gratitude to the American Constitution, but even my brothers and sisters in restricted nations testify to a freedom in Jesus that laws will never nullify. When our right to love Jesus is dependent on the government keeping it safe, we are not worshiping Jesus, we are worshiping our safety.

And, brothers and sisters, as I said earlier, we are not called to be safe. We are called to love. We are called to surrender. We are called to sacrifice. We are called to a willingness to be uncomfortable.

You've probably seen the WWJD bracelets that were popular in the nineties, which I'll admit was a pretty dope concept. I don't think there's anything wrong with asking, "What would Jesus do?" I mean, a lot of life is lived in the gray, so imagining what Jesus might do in a situation and letting that guide our actions can be a great tool. But I would also contend that a lot of life is not as fuzzy or vague as we might imagine, and if we are not careful, we can hypothesize what Jesus *might have done* into a cover for ignoring what He *actually said and did.* Better stated, I'm less interested in what Jesus might do and more interested in what Jesus actually said. Jesus makes it clear: "You are my friends if you do what I command you."[15] And Jesus commands us to love God, to love our neighbors, and to love our enemies. That means being willing at times to forsake our own sense of comfort for the benefit of others. It is time for us to step out of our air-conditioned faith into the heat of reality, secure in the knowledge that God will protect us no matter what comes our way.

I am reminded of the story of Shadrach, Meshach, and Abednego in Daniel 3. King Nebuchadnezzar had just erected a giant golden statue in Babylon and commanded everyone to bow down and worship it or be "thrown into a furnace of blazing fire."[16] For the most part, everyone did as the king commanded—everyone except for three men: Shadrach, Meshach, and Abednego.

Furious, the king summoned the three men and said, "If you don't worship [the image I have made], you will immediately be thrown into a furnace of blazing fire—and who is the god who can rescue you from my power?"[17]

The three men, without flinching, replied, "Nebuchadnezzar, we don't need to give you an answer to this question. If the God we serve exists, then he can rescue us from the furnace of blazing fire, and he can rescue us from the power of you, the king. But even if he does not rescue us, we want you as king to know that we will not serve your gods or worship the gold statue you set up."[18]

So the king had all three men thrown into the furnace, which was so hot it killed the soldiers Nebuchadnezzar had assigned to throw the men in. As Nebuchadnezzar watched the scene unfold before him, he was suddenly struck by something he could not explain. Not only were Shadrach, Meshach, and Abednego moving freely in the furnace unharmed, but there was a fourth person in there with them! Stunned, he called the three men to exit the furnace, and when he saw that not so much as a hair on their heads had been singed, he declared, "Praise to the God of Shadrach, Meshach, and Abednego! He sent his angel and rescued his servants who trusted in him. They violated the king's command and risked their lives rather than serve or worship any god except their own God."[19]

Brothers and sisters, if we are committed to following the commands of Christ, we're going to find ourselves in many, many furnaces. It's unavoidable. But God has promised to save us not *from* the furnace, but *in* the furnace. He is with us in the danger, in the loss, in the pain, in the sacrifice, and in the inconvenience, insulating our souls from incineration. This is Romans 8:38-39: "Neither death nor life, nor angels nor rulers, nor things present nor things to come, nor powers, nor height nor depth, nor any other created thing will be able to separate us from the love of God that is in Christ Jesus our Lord."

So let me ask you . . . is this Jesus stuff real to *you*?

CHAPTER 3

DANGEROUS GOSPEL

**The gospel's more potent than they ever wanted /
The boat can't be sunk when Jesus is sleepin' on it.**
"DARK SKIN"

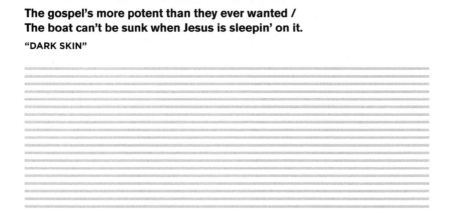

I am a fan of any marketing campaign that makes me say, "Wow, that was genius." Fire designs, compelling stories, witty one-liners—the kinds of things that make me go, "Ah . . . I see what you did there." Needless to say, I get just as excited about the commercials that air during the Super Bowl as I do about the game, because when a company can perfectly weave storytelling, drama, and humor into a thirty-second pitch, that is peak brilliance. The company that constantly kills it is GEICO. You don't even have to use GEICO to know that "fifteen minutes could save you 15 percent or more on car insurance." It also helps that they spend over one billion dollars on ads each year.

When I was in high school, GEICO was running one of my all-time favorites, the "I've got good news" campaign. The commercials were hilarious stories of people getting good news that wasn't close to good enough for the circumstances. One of the commercials was a mock home improvement show. It opens with the host saying, "Welcome back. I'm here in this nineteenth-century Victorian with new owners Mike and Shannon Boyd." The camera pans to Mike and Shannon, who cheerfully respond, "We just fell in love with its charm." To which the host says, "Yeah, it's charming. Unfortunately, the roof leaks, the foundation is crumbling, and there is significant termite damage." The smiles on Mike and Shannon's faces start to fade. Then after a pregnant pause, the host says, "But I *do* have good news. I just saved a bunch of money on my car insurance by switching to GEICO!" He pats them on the back and enthusiastically shows them everything else that is wrong with the lemon they just bought. It's funny (and genius) because it's so ridiculously inappropriate. I mean, if my house is on fire, I don't want you to comfort me with "Look on the bright side—Chipotle is having a two-for-one burrito sale!" Sure, it's good news, but it's not on par with the bad news. Good news is only good if it compensates for the bad news.

I think in some ways GEICO's "gospel"—a word that literally means "good news"—has a striking resemblance to what is commonly called the "gospel" in American Christianity, but instead of car insurance, we're selling soul insurance, helping people secure a place in heaven while completely ignoring the realities of life on earth. The bad news is that sin is ravishing the world around you, breaking your body, and suffocating your community, but hey! The good news is you'll go to heaven when it's done. That gospel is good news, but it doesn't have much of anything to say to the scope of the bad news.

It reminds me of the drug dealer's response to a preacher calling him to leave the hustle and "get saved." The drug dealer looks at him and says, "That sounds good and all, but what are we supposed to eat tonight? My children can't eat your Bible." We cherish the intangible or invisible realities of being forgiven, being made right with God, and being members of the body of Christ, and that is good news.

But in what ways does that good news incarnate for the bad news of our circumstances today?

One of the chief issues with the Christianity of the Land is that its gospel is too small. Though the gospel can be simple, it is also far deeper than we can imagine. It's simple in that it's so straightforward, you can't get around what it's talking about, but it's Mediterranean deep in the reality of its power. It's near and relevant to all those who believe, and yet there is a depth to it that will take an eternity to plunge. Like the ocean, an infant can walk the gospel shores unharmed, yet there are depths that would drown an elephant. Both touch its substance, but neither fully master its scope. All can wade in its shallow waters, but none can fully explore the depths of its reservoir.

While speaking of this good news, English preacher Frank Boreham expounds that "it took all Eternity to arrange, it has the ages of Time as the theater of its operations, and it will take another Eternity to reveal it."[1] We need to realize the gospel is as big as what God is doing in the universe. Like the nature of God Himself, there is always infinitely more to discover.

THE BLACK HOLE IN THE GOSPEL

We are right to say that the gospel is at the center of all that we do. It's the announcement that God has come to rescue the lost from the terrors of Satan, death, and sin. God created men and women in His image to reflect His brilliance and enjoy loving relationship with Him, His world, and one another. But humanity fumbled this offering, sinned against God, and now lives in conflict with God. Because of this, our relationship with the world and each other is crucially broken.

But in steps Jesus! Through His sinless life, sacrificial death, and glorious resurrection, He brings restoration, repair, and redemption to our relationship with God, this world, and others. If we believe in what Jesus has done, we are promised a new life, a victorious death, and eternity in the presence of our good Creator God—setting us free to love others with the love God has shown us in Jesus. This is good news!

As we looked at in chapter 1, one of the reasons Christianity spread so rapidly was that its good news reordered social relationships—outsiders were treated as insiders, women and men served together, slaves became family, and there was a spirit of freedom and equality that contrasted with the Greco-Roman society. This gospel is a beautiful disrupter.

One of the biggest indicators that the Christianity of the Land's gospel does not present the whole picture of this good news is the way that it does not transform the social order; it supports it. We see this in the racial turmoil in our country and in our churches. Racism has routinely become part of the public conversation in America, yet many of our evangelical brothers and sisters would find the conversation to be irrelevant to the gospel.

When Trayvon Martin was killed, some Christians insisted that we talk more about what it means for the gospel to influence the world around us. In other words, what are the social dimensions of the gospel? How does it impact people here and now? Does the gospel involve social justice? For many people in the church, the answer was a resounding no. Police brutality, racial supremacy, racial discrimination—all things that Jesus died to eradicate—are said not to be "gospel issues." These people believe the gospel is exclusively about the salvation of the soul. Christians ought to simply preach the gospel and wait, and maybe as a by-product, we *might* get some change.

Just preach the gospel.

Worry about rescuing people's souls.

Don't concern yourself with their bodies.

Just like the GEICO commercial, we have good news that is too small to compensate for the realities of the bad news. And a spiritually segregated, half-baked gospel is exactly what has historically allowed evil to live alongside religion.

It isn't lost on me that many of the same churches that invite me to proclaim "His glory alone" on their stages today would have been closed or opposed to me just one hundred years ago. The arguments for segregation and racial supremacy have been in the mouths of Christians since the founding of this nation.

It's no surprise that some of the best gospel preachers in American history were slave owners and openly defended the institution of slavery. And in case you think they were simply products of their time, know that there were other men and women in their time that told them they were wrong.

Eighteenth-century clergyman Albert Barnes declared, "You cannot preach the gospel in its purity over the world, without . . . breaking off the shackles of slavery—without making men everywhere free."

And Charles Spurgeon, in his "Separating the Precious from the Vile," said, "Christ's free Church bought with his blood, must bear the shame of cursing Africa, and keeping her sons in bondage."[2]

Not everyone's gospel was shrunken. There were many other Christians—and even some denominations—that were involved in the abolition movement explicitly *because* of their faith. But they were minorities, largely seen as threats to and not champions of the gospel.

Even so, the Southern Baptists started their convention, literally, because they wanted to hold slaves. It wasn't that the Northern Baptists didn't believe in the deity of Christ and they did. It wasn't that they believed in the inspiration of Scripture and the North didn't. It wasn't any of that. They wanted to keep a theological tradition that postured Jesus and slavery as teammates. Period. This is why they seceded and became the Southern Baptist Convention—so that they could keep slavery alive.[3]

And we see the legacy of this profound wickedness with most if not all the major modern-day Christian institutions in the

South—schools, Bible colleges, and seminaries founded on the principle of segregation. Many of them defied the laws of integration of the sixties into the seventies, eighties, and nineties as if it were duty to God. Imagine a gospel so twisted that maintaining white supremacy is perceived as faithfulness to God!

I mean, look at Bob Jones University. Up until the early 2000s, it was committed to keeping its school free of interracial marriage and dating.[4] They were, praise God, the last of a dying breed.

The fact of the matter is, the Jim and Jane Crow South was not a departure from the national vison of our founding fathers. It was the fulfillment. When Thomas Jefferson penned the words "all men are created equal," he was sure to discern that this statement was not a challenge to the "peculiar institution" of slavery and was not at all intended to apply to slaves. It was the Reconstruction Amendments of 1865 to 1870 that rightly reappropriated the biblical idea of equality to non-white individuals. While the idea that we could all live together in racial harmony is a relatively new pursuit for this country, it is not new to God—racial harmony was a key indicator of the power of the early church. Yet in America, often the loudest and too often the discouraging voices in the debates on whether immigrants should be embraced or expelled or whether the issues of minorities deserve national attention are people who identify as Christians.

We saw it all through the antebellum South and during Reconstruction. As people were coming out of slavery, there were efforts, even by the nonbelieving world, to empower former slaves in their newfound freedom. And who were among the most vocal individuals resisting their empowerment? It was people who claimed to be Bible-believing Christians. Even the Ku Klux Klan, the longest-running terrorist group in the United States, postured itself as a Christian movement.

I am always astounded when reading the gospel presentation of men who were so profoundly on the wrong side of righteousness when it came to the question of slavery. Their presentation, as long as they weren't referencing race, was as clear and crisp as one could imagine. They preached Jesus' death, burial, resurrection. "Repent and believe"—amazing stuff! After all, was that not the Good News? Yet these very preachers were standing against the abolition of slavery and the progress of civil rights while telling folks to wait until heaven, where Christ would truly make us equal. These alleged Bible-believing Christians had so segregated the gospel to the sweet by-and-by that it never caused issues with how they treated human beings in the bitter now-and-now.

Their rendition of the gospel spoke strictly to the salvation of souls. It allowed individuals to maintain an eloquent gospel, care less for their neighbors, and sleep fine at night. The legacy of this can be seen in modern platitudes like "it's not a skin issue; it's a sin issue." Sin *makes* skin an issue, so it's not an either-or. It's a skin issue *because* it's a sin issue. Platitudes like that are just nice ways for people to avoid wrestling deeply with the complexity of the works of the enemy in the world. The segregated gospel of the Christianity of the Land allows the evils of the land to live side by side with the gospel itself, not transforming the evils but partnering with them. A gospel that is disconnected from reality has permitted Christians to keep their prejudice, inactivity, apathy, and lack of care for their neighbors while remaining in good standing with the church.

As Oxford scholar Dr. Anthony G. Reddie explains, this disconnected gospel "makes Jesus a non-confrontational, pathetic and nondescript figure who neither has the will nor the desire to effect any semblance of change in the here and now, save for the fact that his death enables people to be 'saved'; but with no accompanying desire for such individuals to change their racist practices or views." Reddie concludes, "Is it any wonder that Black theology did not have any time for this seemingly powerless and pathetic version of Jesus!"[5]

The Christianity of Christ, however, is ruled by the true Jesus and a true message that changes everything. When we turn to the Bible, I believe it's clear that too often we have not been preaching the whole gospel but only pieces of it. The gospel within Scripture is a full gospel. It is not truncated to tight theological aphorisms that point only to future reward. Nah. Jesus' gospel is about invading the messiness of reality, today.

BODY AND SOUL

Perhaps the best way to think about the gospel is simply the Kingdom of God. Mark 1:14-15 says, "After John [the Baptist] was arrested, Jesus went to Galilee, proclaiming the good news [gospel] of God: 'The time is fulfilled, and the kingdom of God has come near. Repent and believe the good news!'" The terms "Kingdom of God" and "Kingdom of Heaven" are found over a hundred times in the New Testament, most densely in the Gospels. And though I love the phrase "gospel of grace and forgiveness," I love all the more the way the Bible uses the phrase "gospel of God." The gospel is *God-big*. This opens things up.

> **TOO OFTEN WE HAVE NOT BEEN PREACHING THE WHOLE GOSPEL BUT ONLY PIECES OF IT. THE GOSPEL WITHIN SCRIPTURE IS A FULL GOSPEL.**

The Kingdom of God is God's undisputed reign. According to the Bible, this heavenly rule is mediated on earth through Christ, and when Jesus says to pray that things would be "on earth as in heaven," He envisions the Kingdom of God, moment by moment, situation by situation, breaking through the darkness of this world. After His death and resurrection, Jesus is not waiting to be Lord. He is Lord now and currently sits at the right hand of the Father, reigning and ruling as we speak, slowly yet certainly seeing to it that the Kingdom of God overwhelms every single aspect of this world.[6] Wherever the works of the enemy are found, the Kingdom of God is hawking them down and making them bow to redemption. I love it!

We, as believers, are to be microcosms of this cosmic redemption.

We have been saved and redeemed, and now the purifying work of the Spirit is making us fit for this coming glory. The Spirit is moving us toward a perfect state. This is the destination of all creation. All creation will reflect the Kingdom of God in its perfection. This is the coming of the new heaven and new earth. This is the gospel—a gospel that is as big as the Kingdom of God, creating right relationships with God, with our neighbors, and with the universe.

The Christianity of the Land rightly puts a premium on piety and the individual's soul being rescued from damnation, but the Christianity of Christ is not satisfied to stop there. There is no such thing as a personal relationship with Christ that does not include personal care for others. The conditions of the soul are connected to the realities of the body. I am reminded of the drug dealer's comments to the preacher that his kids can't eat a Bible. The way God has decided to reveal Himself is through the Word. Have you ever seen what hunger does to a man's or a woman's ability to read? Is hunger not a gospel issue?

The gospel is a profoundly human message. I don't like using the popular church phrase "soul winning" because the Kingdom is not winning souls; it's winning *people*. The gospel is for human beings, which are bodies *and* souls. Jesus did not come to save half of you. He came to save all of you. The redemption of humankind, therefore, is the redemption of both body *and* soul. The gospel of the Kingdom always goes further.

What we see in the Christianity of the Land is the tallying of converts. But the New Testament is not after converts. The New Testament is after disciples. Conversion is a moment where you pray a prayer or confess that you need Christ, which is great! But discipleship encompasses an entire life.

When Christ commissions His disciples, He tells them to teach "them [all nations] to observe everything I have commanded you."[7] Being baptized into the Kingdom, therefore, means not only being made holy and counted righteous before God but also caring for

The New Testament is not after converts. The New Testament is after disciples.

our neighbors and the needy because this is key to the "everything I commanded you."

For far too long, we have been comfortable neglecting the social dimensions of the gospel. But the gospel casts a much wider net than how we have often understood it. So when people say, "Just preach the gospel," I say, "Amen." But we need to preach the *right* gospel, because the *right* gospel includes not only *my* salvation and circumstances but also those of the people around me, because the Kingdom of God encompasses the entire cosmos.

Preaching the gospel means overcoming the works of the enemy wherever they are found. Societal injustice is not a side issue. A gospel that does not care about societies is not the gospel at all. In other words, social dimensions are not merely implications of the gospel; they are inherent to the gospel.

Proclaiming the gospel is indeed the Kingdom of God invading this world. So wherever we run into the reality of sin and systems of oppression, the gospel demands that those things bow down to Jesus. If the gospel fails to address these things, it is no longer the gospel from the Scriptures, because the gospel from the Scriptures moves toward the redemption of all things. This implies that we be active in the societies we live in.

A FULLER GOSPEL

In Matthew 23:23, Jesus calls out the religious leaders because "you pay a tenth of mint, dill, and cumin, and yet you have neglected the more important matters of the law—justice, mercy, and faithfulness." Their involvement with religious piety was important, but Jesus says there are more important dimensions to the redeeming message. He points to justice, mercy, and faithfulness as more important than our individual religious commitments. Let that sink in! It could very well be that reflecting on your morning devotions isn't as weighty as standing up for a mistreated coworker.

Gross injustices like abortion, racism, and economic and environmental insecurity are not extra-credit issues. It is often assumed that what is core to the gospel is simply understanding your soul's justification in light of God's grace demonstrated on the cross, which is true. But how do you know you've actually understood it? The half-baked gospel calls people to *agree* with the gospel, but the gospel of the Kingdom calls people to *obey* the gospel. When the gospel is truncated, it is over-spiritualized, and it fails to help folks see how God's invisible justification relates to our visible efforts.

That is why I have always had a problem with people telling struggling Christians, "Stop trying to do what is right; just surrender to Jesus." Paul says, "Work out your salvation with fear and trembling. For it is God who is working in you both to will and to work."[8] God does powerful things with our attempts to follow Him. Furthermore, the advice to stop trying to help yourself often spills over into not trying to help others either. Though it is true that faith is a gift from God and that we will never be able to save ourselves or to work hard enough to earn God's approval, our work and effort are also gifts from God! Faith is evidenced by people who try to live out what Jesus called us to do—not perfectly, but intentionally. This is what James says: "'You have faith, and I have works.' Show me your faith without works, and I will show you faith by my works."[9] Dallas Willard puts it like this: "Grace is not opposed to effort, but is opposed to earning."[10] This is a much fuller gospel.

There is perhaps no better or more direct example in Scripture that gets at the true meaning of the gospel than the exchange between Jesus and the rich young ruler in Matthew 19. When the rich young ruler asks Jesus what he must do to enter the Kingdom of Heaven, Jesus replies, "If you want to be perfect, go, sell your belongings and give to the poor, and you will have treasure in heaven. Then come, follow me."[11]

Here we have an example of someone in Scripture coming to Jesus—perhaps the most qualified individual to define the gospel—and asking Him what he must do to inherit eternal life. Jesus, in His response, did not say, "You can't do anything; just trust me." Which is true in a sense: Jesus said to His disciples, "Apart from me you can do nothing."[12] But that's not what Jesus says here. Jesus commands the rich young ruler to take everything he has and aim it at the impoverished. Note that Jesus isn't directing him to give to just anybody but specifically to the vulnerable. Jesus isn't teaching salvation by giving to the poor. He is demonstrating that generosity toward the poor has huge implications for whether you actually believe. Jesus is approaching faith not from the angle of dogma ("say yes to these truths") but demonstration ("how ya livin'?").

Brothers and sisters, faith is evidenced by what we do. Our actions give a far more accurate reading of our hearts than our words do. We cannot have a solid faith in God, excel in personal holiness, truly belong to Jesus, and yet be disconnected from social expressions of the gospel. There is no gospel in Scripture that is disconnected from a social dimension because there is no Christian walk in the Bible that is disconnected from other people. As John writes, "If anyone says, 'I love God,' and yet hates his brother or sister, he is a liar. For the person who does not love his brother or sister whom he has seen cannot love God whom he has not seen."[13]

Hate and disregard, as evidenced by injustice, are indeed dangerous, but I promise you this, my brothers and sisters: love is even more dangerous!

WORKIN' IT

While we do not earn our salvation, we do show the gospel's effects in our lives by what we do. We often forget that the first institution God gave to man was not marriage, prayer, or worship. It was gardening—*work*. This makes sense because everything God accomplishes He does through work. He is a worker God. We are to be worker people. We are to be doing His work: "For we are [God's] workmanship, created in Christ Jesus for good works, which God prepared ahead of time for us to do."[14]

Many of our good work opportunities will come to us in our actual workplaces. They must. We spend a third of our lives (roughly ninety thousand hours) at our jobs, so if everyone is to give an account before God of their life, that means one-third of our judgment will involve work. What better opportunity do we have to share the gospel in word and demonstration than by love for our customers, clients, and coworkers? Our jobs are a gospel issue.

Christianity is doing what Jesus did. He came to the world, lived among us, and assumed all of the virtues that identify true religion—the act of loving, the act of healing, the act of caring, and the act of teaching—all for this opportunity for the world to see and glorify the Father in heaven as a result of us imitating His actions. As I said before, I cannot overstate that our work does not *earn* us God's favor, but God's favor is often confirmed by what He does through our hands and feet.

Consider Matthew 25:31-46, Jesus' words concerning separating sheep from goats. The sheep—"the righteous"—will go "into eternal life," while the goats "will go away into eternal punishment." What was the differentiating evidence, in Jesus' eyes, between the goats and the sheep? Work:

> Come, you who are blessed by my Father; inherit the kingdom prepared for you from the foundation of the world.
> For I was hungry and you gave me something to eat; I was thirsty and you gave me something to drink; I was a stranger and you took me in; I was naked and you clothed me; I was sick and you took care of me; I was in prison and you visited me.[15]

Christ enthusiastically rewards those whose actions reflect His Kingdom. He doesn't praise them for *sharing* the gospel; He praises them for *being* the gospel!

Here is a sobering question for us all to consider: If those who call themselves Christians disappeared, would anyone notice? Or worse yet, would the world be better off? God forbid!

Os Guinness, who has written extensively on calling, writes, "The problem with Western Christians is not that they aren't where they should be but that they aren't what they should be where they are."[16]

I would argue that we don't just need more pastors and theologians who teach the true gospel for impact to be felt across our country. I contend that we need more lawyers. We need more doctors. We need more artists. We need more educators. We need more police officers, more bus drivers, more nonprofit workers, more nurses, more entrepreneurs, more senators, governors, mayors, accountants, authors, directors, screenwriters, and producers loving their neighbors and actively doing the Lord's work! We need to be sharing the gospel, loving God, and loving others right where we are, in the workplaces where God has placed us.

DANGEROUS GOSPEL

In order to be a true threat to evil, the gospel must encompass redemption, justification, sanctification, salvation, and glorification. Not one of these pieces is the entirety of the gospel—all are interconnected. Whenever we make one of these things the entirety of the gospel, we lose the true scope, depth, and breadth of the gospel.

If we make grace the entirety of the gospel, for example, then we might slip into antinomianism, believing the law of God is irrelevant. But Jesus says to His disciples, "If you love me, you will keep my commands. . . . The one who has my commands and keeps them is the one who loves me. And the one who loves me will be loved by my Father. I also will love him and will reveal myself to him."[17]

Similarly, if we make redemption the exclusive indicator of the gospel, then we are left with a purely social gospel unconcerned about people's eternal state. Advocating for a full stomach for the hungry without addressing the emptiness of the soul can better people's condition today—at the risk of ignoring their eternal destiny.

If justification is the whole gospel, then like some of the Puritans, people can have devotions in their front yard while the clinking and clattering of chains is echoing from the fields. If the gospel is merely about justification, then the chaplain on the slave ship has no need to worry about the physical reality of chattel slavery as long as he has preached salvation to the slave's soul.

If sanctification is everything, then all we focus on is how we can avoid sin and are left utterly devastated when we fail. When this happens, not only do we become hyper-focused on personal performance, but we also fail to see that Christ will always have more grace to give than we have sin to commit.

If glorification or the new heavens and new earth are all there is, then we run the risk of becoming fatalistic. Whatever happens, happens; we'll die and go to heaven one day.

If any one of these aspects is elevated as the whole gospel while leaving out the others, ultimately the gospel is compromised. Only when all components are honored can the Good News be fully realized.

I often contemplate what the world might look like if those who name Jesus as Lord obeyed His gospel with their whole hearts. Jesus said to love our neighbors as we love ourselves, full stop. Do we really need any other condemnation of slavery? Do we really need any other impetus to care about immigrants, the homeless, the addicted? Loving our neighbors should cover the entire gamut. This human being—*every* human being— is a neighbor. We are to treat them how *we* would want to be treated.

However, if the salvation of the soul replaces the importance of the condition of the body, then we can flip this on its head and say, "I understand this person doesn't deserve neighborly love, but the big thing is that we loved him by winning him to Jesus." And somehow people are okay with that. But in reality, they are distorting the gospel. How can we explain God's love *for* the world while maintaining that God isn't really concerned about loving people while they are *in* the world?

OUR JOB IS NOT TO MAKE THE GOSPEL MORE RELEVANT TO PEOPLE. THE GOSPEL IS RELEVANT BECAUSE PEOPLE ARE SINNERS.

Our job is not to make the gospel more relevant to people. The gospel is relevant because people are sinners. But sin, as we understand it, is an affront to God and a destroyer of His world. And the Bible makes it clear that the way we know we are offending God vertically is how things are playing out horizontally. It's my pride toward other people that elevates my humanity over them. It's my greed that puts profit over people. It's my sinful ambition that causes me to keep up with the Joneses as opposed to giving more to those in need. I often say what it means for me to be a Christian is that I will never have as much money as I could have had if I wasn't one, because loving Jesus means caring about the needs of others along with my own.

This, brothers and sisters, is why the gospel is relevant. Sin is earthly. It's human. It shows itself in the form of bias, evil, anger, lust, fornication, and adultery. Almost every sin we have in the Bible has a tangible reality to it. Sin is not disembodied from earthly reality. Neither is our gospel.

Paul calls Satan "the god of this world,"[18] but God is supreme over Satan. And this world is filled with God's glory—a glory that is overcoming the ugliness of the present age via our preaching the gospel and caring for God's world. The gospel is the Kingdom of God coming to earth, and obeying the gospel is exercising Kingdom reality in everyday life. This is why we have a heart for the immigrant community, and orphans, and the impoverished. This is why our hearts break when we witness or learn about injustices. It's our gospel inheritance. This is the good-dangerous gospel of the Christianity of Christ.

CHAPTER 4
DANGEROUS CITIZEN

Yes, I love the kingdom more than I love my nation. / Yes, I love my
neighbor more than I love his papers.

"LONG LIVE THE CHAMPION"

I will never forget the first time I saw my son sing in public. Michelle
and I were sitting in the church sanctuary with about two hundred
other proud parents watching a special performance put on by his
school.

Now, I should mention that Michelle and I were very intentional
about choosing the right school for KBJ. It wasn't just about aca-
demics (though that was an important consideration). We wanted
to know the culture of the institution. Did it have a diverse ethnic
background? Was character development central to the curriculum?
Was the environment hostile toward belief in God? So when we
found a well-reviewed Christian school near our home and church
that seemed to check all our boxes, we felt like we had hit the lotto!
Well . . . almost. When we went to scope it out, we found the school
wanting in diversity (KBJ was the only black kid in his class), but

we felt that the emphasis on Jesus and the diversity of our own community would make up for it, so we rolled with it.

At the concert, the students were performing in order by grade, so KBJ's preschool class was up first. As the kids filed in, I sat up a little straighter, excited to find out if little KBJ was a chip off the old block. After all, Daddy's got a little song and dance ability in his blood.

KBJ's class had a Noah's ark theme going, so all the kids were dressed up like animals. Looking over the herd, I saw KBJ. He was easy to spot—it was like looking at a speck of pepper in a snowstorm. Thankfully, KBJ was dressed as a lion. I leaned over to Michelle and whispered, "At least they didn't make him the monkey." Thank the Lord for small favors.

Now, as an artist, I love live performances, and I have to intentionally choose not to be a snob. But as soon as they finished singing, I couldn't help it. I leaned over to my wife and said, "That was a little rough."

"KB," she gently reminded me, "they are five years old."

"I know. I just expected more."

I was just joking of course. There's something about watching five-year-olds sing off-key and clap offbeat that ministers to my soul. Even so, there *was* something about the performance that bothered me. It was not how they sang but what they were singing about.

For over an hour, I watched each class present two songs—one about allegiance to Jesus ("Jesus Loves Me," "This Little Light of Mine," "I've Got the Joy, Joy, Joy, Joy," etc.) directly followed by a song about allegiance to the United States ("America the Beautiful," "My Country 'Tis of Thee," "This Land Is Your Land," etc.).

There we were, standing in the sanctuary of a house of worship, commending America as much as Jesus. Now, I don't have a problem with kids singing "America the Beautiful," but what was concerning was that after an hour of singing songs about love for God directly adjacent to songs about love for country, they started to sound like the same song. What started off as an adorable performance of tone-deaf children (I'm sorry; I can't help it) started to feel like the seeds of an age-old idolatry, making the line between God and country so thin that "God *and* country" starts to feel more like "God *is* country." And that is a much worse kind of tone deafness.

ONE NATION, UNDER GOD

One of the most consequential flaws of the Christianity of the Land is its complicity in making an idol out of the United States. Folks won't bluntly say, "God bless America . . . and nowhere else," but really, how much are we asking God to bless anywhere else?

This idea is known as nationalism. Nationalism goes beyond mere patriotism in that it turns pride in one's country into a religion. American journalist Sydney Harris wrote, "The difference between patriotism and nationalism is that the patriot is proud of his country for what it does, and the nationalist is proud of his country no matter what it does; the first attitude creates a feeling of responsibility, but the second a feeling of blind arrogance."[1]

With nationalism, the reputation of the nation becomes so sacred that criticism of its excellence is like an act of treason. Politicians become like priests and saviors with the salvation of the country in their hands. Meanwhile, "othered" groups like refugees, immigrants, and minorities are often marginalized, seen as job thieves and criminals. But when we consider the phrase "America first," does it apply to all Americans? Does the mantra go to bat for Japanese Americans, Mexican Americans, or Native Americans? Not to say that having a special affinity for people in your country is problematic. Paul said in Romans 9 that he has unique longing for his people "according to the flesh."[2] The distinction lies in what that love means for outsiders. Or, as Charles de Gaulle once said, "Patriotism is when love of your own people comes first; nationalism, when hate for people other than your own comes first."

And let's keep it real. Nationalism often finds itself in bed with racism because it demands we preserve what *was*, and it fears the "face of America" changing into something less European. Nationalism doesn't always mean racism, but it is certainly the favored flavor of racists. The prospect of Americans speaking other languages ("Speak English!"), protecting the human rights of non-Christian people ("Ban Muslims!"), and the fifty-year projection that white people will be the minority in America is terrifying to this belief.

NATIONALISM GOES TO CHURCH

As I said, the Christianity of the Land is complicit in propping up idolatrous worship of the United States in what has been called "Christian nationalism." I hit up author and researcher Andrew Whitehead, coauthor of *Taking America Back for God*, and asked him to crystallize in a sentence what the promised land is for Christian nationalism. He told me, "Christian nationalism desires a society where white natural-born citizens who are culturally and politically conservative occupy the unquestioned center of the culture and dominate access to political and social power." That is the definition of success in Christian nationalist thought.

When nationalism goes to church, it typically gives birth to what my best friend and podcast cohost Ameen "the Dream" Hudson calls "Patriot Jesus," a power-grabbing, America-focused, neighbor-ignoring Jesus that looks less like a savior and more like a politician, a Jesus that is a figment of Western imagination.

Patriot Jesus has a lot of disciples in this country. Patriot Jesus needs votes, elections, and the promises of politicians to stay viable because He is not powered by the Spirit of the living God but by Washington, DC. After all, why do you need the power of heaven when you are promised the power of the state?

Christian nationalists do not look to preachers and pastors to bring revival to the culture. Their hope lies in politicians. The Jesus of the Bible is not running the show. He's at best a mascot for the team, used to boost popularity but ignored when His commands are too inconvenient. The thing about mascots, though, is that they are always caricatures—distorted reflections of the real thing. And they aren't integral to the operation of the team. There isn't a mascot on the planet that has danced his team into a victory. Sadly, that's what Patriot Jesus is for a large swath of professing Christians in this country, and as a result, there is an incestuous relationship between the Christianity of the Land and American politics that informs how people think, what they do, and how they feel.

One way I've seen this play out is, too often, when would-be prophets start thinking about the end times, it's heavily in relationship to bad things happening in America. In other words, Jesus wasn't coming soon when Ebola hit West Africa. That was just Ebola hitting West Africa. But when COVID-19 happened here, or terrorist attacks happen here, we start talking Armageddon, because the metric for what God is doing everywhere is what He's doing in America.

It is a perverted love for the land that leads us to see America as the primary focus of heaven. No matter how much we behave like Babylon, we see ourselves as Israel, the true location of God's chosen people. The Bible has not taught us that; we have created that identity out of our own sense of exceptionalism.

IT IS A PERVERTED LOVE FOR THE LAND THAT LEADS US TO SEE AMERICA AS THE PRIMARY FOCUS OF HEAVEN.

Let's be clear. Love for our nation is a good thing. God tells His people in Babylon to "pursue the well-being of the city I have deported you to. Pray to the *Lord* on its behalf, for when it thrives, you will thrive."[3] I wouldn't call Jesus a patriot, but He is definitely loving on Nazareth by keeping the city in His name for all eternity. So I'm not opposed to patriotism. What I'm opposed to is when love for country is perverted into a weapon against nonnationals or anyone who is not nationalist enough.

When Jesus says, "If anyone comes to me and does not hate his own father and mother, wife and children, brothers and sisters—yes, and even his own life—he cannot be my disciple,"[4] that is not a typo. Jesus uses *hate*—not literally but as a figure of speech—to show us that love for Jesus is to dominate love for anything else. Your most cherished assets—life, family, and yes, your country—are to exist as subjects, not rivals or substitutes for the Lord Jesus Christ. This isn't Jesus being a jerk; this is Jesus ordering our loves by removing the biggest obstacle to human flourishing: turning good things into God things.

MANIFEST DESTINY

The concept of Christian nationalism is not new. In fact, the idea goes all the way back to the founding fathers, many of whom were Christians. The very doctrine of Manifest Destiny inferred that God has a unique vision and plan for America to thrive as His tabernacle.

I've tapped Southside Rabbi Ameen "the Dream Machine" Hudson to help me sharpen this point. He writes, "There is a baked-in cultural assumption that the 'specialness' of America is so dear to God that the success of the United States is a central part of God's plan. This dynamic is not new. Many of America's forefathers built this country believing God's hand of blessing was on them to bring good fortune to their endeavors. And for centuries, many have attributed America's superpower status to God's favor." In other words, a win for America—no matter how bloodily achieved—is necessarily a win for God.

So what's wrong with believing God's hand is on your country's endeavors? On the face of it, nothing. But when God's perceived blessing on your country comes at the expense of other people's annihilation, subjugation, and oppression, that belief violates the very nature of divine blessings.

One of the more powerful examples of this mentality is America's overthrow of the peaceable Hawaiian Kingdom in 1893. Hawaii, posing no threat whatsoever to the United States, was believed to be of too much military and economic benefit to the United States to allow its ownership by non-Americans.

Princess Ka'iulani, who was to be queen before the American invasion, tried to convince the American people not to do this evil thing. Traveling to the United States to fight against what she saw as a terrible injustice, she gave this speech on her arrival:

> Seventy years ago, Christian America sent over Christian men and women to give religion and civilization to Hawaii. Today, three of the sons of those missionaries are at your capitol asking you to undo their fathers' work. Who sent them? Who gave them the authority to break the Constitution which they swore they would uphold? Today, I, a poor weak girl with not one of my people with me and all these "Hawaiian" statesmen against me, have strength to stand up for the rights of my people. Even now, I can hear their wail in my heart and it gives me strength and courage and I am strong—strong in the faith of God, strong in the knowledge that I am right, strong in the strength of seventy million people who in this free land will hear my cry and will refuse to let their flag cover dishonor to mine![5]

This was a moving appeal to the "Christian" conscience of the American people in an era that is often referred to as "the good ol' days." Princess K got some support but was largely overwhelmed and silenced with racist remarks and heartless threats. The United States proceeded to annex her country, driving native Hawaiians to the less-desirable portions of the island to make room for the American military and taxable tourist income.

What is fascinating about this story is that this wicked effort of erasing Hawaii was greatly facilitated by Christian missionaries.

Even Princess K's appeal to her own faith in Jesus was eclipsed by Christians committed to their faith in their nation's interest.

What the Bible teaches about stealing, killing, bearing the image of God, having inalienable rights to exercise dominion over the land, plus the special incentive to prioritize the "household of faith" has a tendency to go flying out the window if it means America isn't first. Again, a win for America, no matter how bloody and godlessly achieved, is a win for God!

The US Congress apologized in 1993, acknowledging that "the overthrow of the Kingdom of Hawaii . . . [occurred] with the participation of agents and citizens of the United States," and that "the indigenous Hawaiian people never directly relinquished their claims to their inherent sovereignty as a people or over their national lands to the United States,"[6] but the Hawaiian people are still largely disenfranchised to this day.[7]

We often ignore the power of legacy. It is easy to look back on history and think, *We would never.* More often than not, the reality is that we already have.

THE IMMORAL MAJORITY

On January 6, 2021, in an act of terror, a group of American citizens stormed the United States Capitol in an attempt to overturn the results of the 2020 presidential election. What was striking about the insurrection was how often its members referenced Jesus. At one point in the middle of the madness, someone led a prayer of thanksgiving and victory on the floor of the House of Representatives that they had just violently overrun.

This insurrection was the overflow of something that had been brewing since the 2016 election, when scores of Christians and Christian institutions got behind Donald Trump's presidential bid, implying that he was "God's man for America" and that he was going to bring the country back to God, even though he himself was a prideful, profane, materialistic, self-styled playboy who had publicly expressed he had never asked for God's forgiveness. Most evangelicals condemned these actions, but that doesn't mean we were off the hook. Studies showed that Christians (largely white evangelicals) did not believe that Christian morals were necessary to be a good leader, making Christian morals à la carte as long as it meant winning. This thought was absolutely bewildering to the onlooking world.

Prominent Christian leader John MacArthur said in a 2016 panel discussion,

> Remember the moral majority, when morals meant something? And now we have a guy running for president being advocated by Christian university presidents and pastors who is a public adulterer . . . multiple marriages? Does family mean anything? Does anybody care about family? When you've lived with women who weren't your wife while you were married to other ones, then paraded your sexual exploits in a book? So what happened to the moral majority? Evangelicals used to be equated with the moral majority. Morality doesn't define us anymore.[8]

MacArthur had a tremendous effect on my life when I first became a Christian, so it was disheartening that by the time the 2020 election rolled around, MacArthur had completely switched jerseys, taking his talents down to Mar-a-Lago. He stated in an interview that he told Donald Trump personally that "any real, true believer is going to be on your side in this election," seeming to suggest that support for Donald Trump was tantamount to faithfulness.[9] Now I got love for Johnny Mac, but our moral witness taking a back seat to the agenda of saving the country from the opposing political party is an act of fear, not faith.

Other leaders theologized MacArthur's assumption. Leaders like

Pastor Robert Jeffress frequently spun arguments to support Trump's moves, like saying that "Heaven itself is gonna have a wall around it" to support Trump's wall at the southern border.[10] Paula White, prosperity gospel preacher turned White House spiritual adviser, said that God had "raised up" Donald Trump and that to resist him was to fight against the "hand of God."[11] Still other leaders encouraged Christians to vote for Trump by saying that something greater than the reputation of the church and the future of the country was at stake. That's not to say that every instance of Christians supporting Donald Trump—or any candidate, for that matter—is Christian nationalism. There are many good reasons to support a leader that don't equate to idolatry. I am specifically addressing those instances when it does. Any support of an elected official is support for a sinner, so there is plenty of grace for us at the ballot box. What is indeed troublesome is when we punt our public witness and justify what deserves to be denounced. We, of all people, must not "trust in princes, in a son of man, in whom there is no salvation."[12] Instead, we must "trust in the LORD forever, because in the LORD, the LORD himself, is an everlasting rock!"[13]

WHAT DOES A CHRISTIAN NATION LOOK LIKE?

I'm convinced the Christianity of the Land doesn't care about making Christian disciples as much as it does about fighting for Christian preferences. It's not as much concerned about winning hearts as it's concerned about winning compliance. In an attempt to avoid persecution, to avoid sharing space with people we think are wrong, and to avoid not being hailed as the religion of the land, the Christianity of the Land will make any adjustment necessary to be seen as the top dog. It's a fight for dominance based on fear and

> **WHAT IS TROUBLESOME IS WHEN WE PUNT OUR PUBLIC WITNESS AND JUSTIFY WHAT DESERVES TO BE DENOUNCED.**

insecurity, displayed in a willingness to do whatever is needed to protect ourselves. Now, we rightfully appreciate religious liberty and our ability to use our Christian voice. But those things can become idols in themselves. And the Christianity of Christ is never dependent on them. The Christianity of Christ has always been fueled by the persuasion of the Spirit over the might of the state.

I am also convinced that the reason many Western Christians have, historically, been unfazed by the world's cry of hypocrisy—pointing out how we excuse the inexcusable in our public leaders—is because public witness is not a priority. It's not as important to be winsome or persuasive as it is to be powerful. It doesn't matter how Christians look to the outside world when our guy is winning. There is no sin that success can't atone for.

This is not okay, nor is it biblical. The Jesus of the Bible has one nation: His people. He has one political interest: His Kingdom. We become citizens of this Kingdom through faith in Him. God's number one priority is His glory and the advancement of His Kingdom.[14] No earthly nation, including the United States, has a monopoly on God's favor and blessing. God is not trying to make a name for a country; He is making a name for Himself!

If a hundred years from now Spanish is the official language of America, the language of love in the Kingdom has lost nothing. If a hundred years from now America is not seen as a "city on a hill" among the nations, the glory of God will not have lost a single lumen of brilliance. As much as I pray God preserves my country, I must realize that God is still God without democracy. He was God before democracy, and He will be God after. Every great nation will be a footnote in the story of redemption our God is writing. Nations die; the Kingdom does not.

We are not wrong to want greatness for our nation. But whose greatness do we really want—ours or His? Because the greatness of Christ is not measured in economic gains, military might, or partisan W's; it is measured in love for God, growth in reflecting Jesus, and care for our neighbors. Economic gains and military might have merit and utility, but they could be perfectly realized and a nation still be utterly abandoned by God (see Babylon). Contrary to popular belief, prosperity is not the key indicator of the presence of God. Greatness is realized when Kingdom priorities intersect with our national priorities. I think former president Jimmy Carter said it well: "The measure of a society is found in how they treat their weakest and most helpless citizens."[15] It is not found in the power and might of its stock market.

The goal of the Christianity of Christ is dual citizenship. The Bible states it clearly: "Our citizenship is in heaven, and we eagerly wait for a Savior from there, the Lord Jesus Christ."[16] We eagerly wait for no one like we wait for our Savior. More than any other affiliation, we want people to know we are *more* than Americans. We are His.

BRINGING HEAVEN DOWN

I live in a neighborhood that's predominantly Indian. You would only need to walk down the street to encounter the presence and spirit of India in my community. You can smell the spices and see folks wearing saris and religious necklaces. From the color and the art to the language and the accents, India is among us. Because India is in my neighbors, they bring India wherever they go.

Once, my neighbor Raj brought a dish over that was so delicious, I texted him, "That's it. I'm moving to India!" He texted me back, "No need. We brought India to you."

This is how dual citizenship in the Kingdom of God is supposed to work. In how we walk and how we talk, all of our customs and practices should have the aroma of heaven. We are not *in* heaven, but heaven is in us, so we should bring heaven wherever we go. When Raj brought that delicious meal, my knee-jerk reaction was, "Take me to the source! I need more!" We are designed to be plates of heaven that we deliver to our neighbors in hopes that they, too, will look to the source.

When Jesus taught the disciples how to pray in Mathew 6, He instructed them to call for God's "will [to] be done on earth as it is in heaven."[17] Jesus made it clear that our primary function in this world is to bring heaven down. We do this by seeking to transform the world in a way that represents the ethics and the reality of the Kingdom of God. This is why we take justice seriously. This is why we take protecting the unborn seriously. This is why we take feeding the hungry and caring for the poor seriously. This is why we take treating the immigrant with respect seriously. This is why we want to see reform in politics that goes beyond Democrats and Republicans to a Kingdom ethic.

Jesus was constantly challenged to give His support to the conservative Pharisees, the liberal Sadducees, or the imperial Romans. All of them got *some* of His support, but none of them got *all* of His support. No nation's agenda is large enough to encompass the agenda of the Kingdom citizen.

If your wagon is hitched to Jesus, you will inevitably find yourself agreeing, intersecting, and aligning with all kinds of movements and political camps as you travel through this world. But rest assured, at some point, Jesus is going to complicate things and possibly get you kicked out!

There is a socialist African American movement that is very active on the south side of St. Petersburg in meeting the needs of the impoverished. They opened a community center and gym, they're helping to feed and educate folks, and they stand up against racial injustice. So I walked into the community center one day, and they gave me a tour of the place and talked about a lot of things they were doing to empower the community. I was super encouraged. It felt like we were kindred spirits in a lot of ways. I said, "Hey, whenever y'all do community events, I'm down with it. Count me in." Then I popped the Jesus question. "So, where are y'all at when it comes to God? I'm deeply committed to Jesus and strongly believe all our effort needs to have a supernatural component to it, you know what I mean?"

And as soon as I brought Jesus into the mix, all the love I had felt before was just . . . *gone.* They were looking at me like, *How in the world could you be this smart and be so brainwashed?* They proceeded to give me game, telling me that Jesus is the white man's invention and talking about colonization and how Jesus was used to enslave our people.

I fired back, "First of all, I haven't been brainwashed. I *have* been washed—by the blood of Jesus Christ." While unnecessary Jesus juke is a second language for me, what I really said was, "Truth be told, my ancestors in North Africa were essential in the spread of Christianity to the West, not to mention the overwhelming commitment the enslaved African church had to Jesus. Then there was the whole Civil Rights era, almost exclusively led by Black Christians. To be honest, I think I'm being more faithful to my ancestors than y'all are."

Needless to say, I was not welcomed back after that conversation.

Brothers and sisters, we will never be conservative enough, liberal enough, or woke enough to be truly at home in any of the world's circles. There is only one place where we are truly at home, and that is in God's Kingdom. But it is precisely our dual citizenship that should make us the unsung assets of whatever spaces we find ourselves in, because we can speak both inside and outside of those camps with transcendental truths. Our bias should be to righteousness. That's our only dog in the fight. Just like loving God over people makes us better lovers of people, so too does being a good citizen of heaven make you a better citizen of this world.

THE REAL BATTLEFIELD

Allegiance to Jesus should not fit perfectly with your allegiance to America. Your allegiance to Jesus should challenge, define, and

We will
never be
conservative
enough,
liberal enough,
or woke enough
to be truly
at home in
any of the
world's
circles.

clarify your allegiance to America. That is what it means to love your country.

Christian nationalism has a very short fuse when it comes to criticizing America, even though many of those criticisms are attempts to improve the country. To the Christian nationalist, a less racist, less misogynistic, less unequal society is less appealing than America looking flawless. It's the "public witness" that absorbs most of the concern.

American writer and activist James Baldwin said, "I love America more than any other country in the world, and, exactly for this reason, I insist on the right to criticize her perpetually."[18]

Nothing should be more patriotic than speaking the ugly truth about America's incestuous relationship with white supremacy while fighting to make her better. If Christians are angry at the idea that most of our founding fathers were racist, it should be because they hate racism, not because it makes America look bad.

Love for America that lies about its history, exalts its victories, and sweeps its failures under the rug is not love that serves our neighbors well. Accountability is an act of love. The Kingdom agenda doesn't just want the nation to look good; it demands that people *be* good. That is what dangerous citizenship looks like.

There is so much value in democracy. Having traveled the world, I am so grateful for America's free and fair elections and the idea of law and order. However, the job of the dual citizen is not simply to outlaw our enemies; it's to love and persuade them. When it comes to moving the heart of a nation, the strongest tool the Christianity of Christ has is not partnership with politicians but partnership with the church. Love, service, sacrifice, and truth-telling are far more persuasive than the sword.

If we politicize those who sit opposite from us, then we cannot appreciate anything good about who they are. We can disagree with LGBTQ sexual ethics, but can't we also bless their desire to protect the trans and queer community from harm? We don't have to agree with the claims of Islam, but can our hearts not break at

Muslims being persecuted and harassed? If I see those I disagree with as humans to be persuaded, not political opponents to be owned, I open myself up to win a person, not a debate.

Every social movement in the last 150 years to bring equal rights to women and minorities and safety to immigrants has been resisted by nationalists, including those who call themselves Christian. And even though the children of these folks realize their parents were wrong, they often live out some iteration of their folly.

The Christianity of Christ breaks this folly through heavenly citizenship guiding our citizenship on earth. We must not get those backward. Do not buy into the lie that various "culture wars" are the true battlefield. The true battlefield is reflecting Jesus to a world that desperately needs Him.

We wrestle not in the power of flesh and blood or partisan politics but in a much greater spiritual reality—the Kingdom reality.

CHAPTER 5

DANGEROUS JUSTICE

Justice in my veins.
"LINCOLN"

In the summer of 2018, I released a Latin-trap track titled "Long Live the Champion" (LLTC). The song, produced by my dear friend Boricua super producer Cardec Drums, intentionally weds the classic vibes of salsa with the grit and punch of 808s. When Cardec sent me the beat through a text message, after a single listen, I could only respond with fire and Latin dance lady emojis!

Folks that know my sound can tell you of my love for blending genres and colliding musical worlds through song. Whether it's hip-hop fused with worship, Latin with gospel, or jazz with trap, I like my music as diverse as the world I make it for. I think this represents who I am. I have served in a multiethnic, multinational, multigenerational, working-class community in Tampa for fifteen years. My friends, brothers, and sisters are Australian, Nigerian, Ghanaian, African American, British, Filipino, Chinese, Caribbean, and Central and South American, to shout out a few. My wife is Panamanian. Her father is Afro-Colombian/Panamanian, and our children are so complicatedly diverse that when people ask us, "What's their ethnicity?" it's easier to just say, "They're human." My community is like a gumbo or its Latin cousin, sancocho: many different ingredients gathered together without erasing the identity of the parts. And the uniqueness of the parts makes a better whole, creating something new and more compelling than the parts by themselves. Jesus has brought us together.

One of the ingredients that the parts bring to the whole is the unique way this present evil age presses against their existence. That is why, in all my music, I try to reflect not just the parts' sounds but also the parts' stories.

Around the time Cardec and I began working on LLTC, many of my Latino brothers and sisters were the target of public scorn. The presidential administration at the time had launched an initiative to purge the country of undocumented immigrants, citing their presence as a core threat to American life. They were assumed to be stealing jobs and bringing drugs and rapists into the country, and this call for "law and order" resonated loudly with many who were already furious about (and scared of) globalization. What followed was an explosion of hostility, the questioning of brown-skinned citizens' citizenship, and perpetual calls to "Go back to your own country."

Many of my friends were living in terror—families who attend annual check-ins at the local immigration office, pay their taxes, own property, pastor churches, and run businesses that have been living in our community "undocumented" for years. Undocumented, by the way, does not necessarily mean the person entered the country illegally. Often it means the person is pursuing permanent residency or citizenship, which can be a very long and expensive process. Regardless, families that were once contributing to and living safely within our community under federal protection were now extremely vulnerable to deportation.

Although immigrants come from everywhere, there was a special concern from this administration about those coming from the Global South. (Immigrants from places like Sweden were encouraged to keep coming.) Studies have shown that these immigrants actually fuel the economy and, of course, have no more unique predilection toward lawlessness than any other group of humans.[1] But none of that stopped the efforts to end America's long-standing legacy of embracing refugees and harboring asylum seekers, people who are fleeing persecution, famine, and war. This included an attempt to end DACA (Deferred Action for Childhood Arrivals), which would have deported more than 700,000 immigrants and refugees who arrived in the United States as children, dropping these children off in countries they've never known. (The attempt to end DACA was later ruled illegal.)

All of this reached critical mass when the attorney general announced the "zero tolerance" policy that aimed to separate children from their parents at the southern border. The comment about the policy that came out of a justice department meeting was "we need to take away children" . . . no matter how young.[2] This was an effort to send a message to the Global South: "You are not welcome here. Figure it out where you are."

Now, this struggle is not unique to our lifetime or limited to any administration. Since Ellis Island, every administration has struggled to reflect a Kingdom image of stranger-welcoming. And our God is a protector; the impulse to protect can be healthy and right, and I understand that doing so while still welcoming those who are outside is a complicated matter. I'm not a politician; I'm a minister of the gospel, and I know these matters are not easy.

But here's what I'm saying about the real-life effect on people living on the ground. To nobody's surprise, the FBI reported that hate crimes had surged by 20 percent. The culprits were mainly white supremacist groups and the victims mainly minority communities. Toxic attitudes toward immigrants and people of color flooded the

Internet: "Go back to your country." "Speak English; this is America." "Jews will not replace us." Hate-filled YouTube and Instagram videos went viral almost daily. So when Cardec and I were creating LLTC, it was crystal clear to me that I needed a record that would speak to these issues with biblical conviction and compassion.

With lyrics like "Weep before you speak, think before you eat. / How you love a country's food more than its people?" and "I have met the bravest / Where they still sing when they living through the anguish," LLTC was designed to celebrate the courage, value, and humanity of the vulnerable—the people who are often celebrated for their food and vacation resorts but rejected when they are in need.

A dear sister named Maria, a DACA-protected Colombian immigrant who moved to the states when she was nine months old, published a tear-jerking response to the song. She writes, "Despite living in the U.S. essentially my whole life, my only identity to many has been 'illegal immigrant.' . . . My identity has always been a source of confusion for me." She writes of the difficulty of knowing how to fill out authorization paperwork for jobs and understanding her place in America. But since meeting Jesus, she has "come to learn that all of us are made in the image of God, no matter what dehumanizing titles and policies come our way. . . . In a country where I constantly carry my documents to prove the worthiness of my residence, I'm so thankful for fellow Christians like KB who boldly proclaim, 'Yes, I love the Kingdom more than I love my nation. Yes, I love my neighbor more than I love his papers.'"[3]

HATRED GONE VIRAL

By God's grace, most of my audience loved the song, and it even landed a T-Mobile commercial, but there was still a significant portion of my audience that was upset I had decided to speak to this subject. This was discouraging but not surprising, as many Christians, either through ignorance or indifference, do not think the vulnerability of the immigrant community is relevant to the gospel.

In fact, a *Washington Post*/ABC poll found that a staggering 75 percent of white evangelicals in the United States, which comprises a significant portion of my following, described "the federal crackdown on undocumented immigrants" as a positive thing, compared to just 46 percent of Americans overall.[4] And according to a Pew Research Center poll, 68 percent of white evangelicals say that America has no responsibility to house refugees, which is a full 25 points higher than the national average.[5]

It's important to say that white evangelicals do not represent all white people, all white Christians, or all Christians in general. The term is for distinction, not dismissal (even though it has been used uncharitably in the media), because white evangelicals are the only Christian group to express this level of hostility toward refugees. While just 25 percent of them say they think Americans *should* house refugees, between 43 and 65 percent of white mainline Protestants, Black Protestants, and Catholics all express support for refugees.[6] Meanwhile, according to another poll by the Public Religion Research Institute, more than half of white evangelicals report feeling concerned about America's declining white population.[7]

My audience is almost exclusively Christian, so it makes sense that I'd be met with some level of resistance. I just didn't anticipate it being quite so toxic.

As part of the release of LLTC, we ran a campaign that included a call to support an organization serving immigrant children and focusing our attention on God's heart for migrant communities.

In preparation for this campaign, I reposted a video to my Facebook feed from a bipartisan organization that brilliantly highlighted the troubling realities these immigrant children faced as they were separated from their parents and forced to defend themselves in immigration court.

The video was a reenactment using transcripts from real court cases of children as young as two years old defending themselves in court. Many of these children came seeking asylum, and since they are not US citizens, they do not have the right to an attorney, so they are left crying in a courtroom while a judge asks them questions like "Do you have a lawyer?" "Do you know where you are?" and "Do you understand immigration law?"

I first watched this video in utter heartbreak because at the time I had a two-year-old, and I could not imagine KBJ being subjected to such circumstances. I wrote in the caption of the video, "This breaks my heart."

As the Scriptures say, "Out of the abundance of the heart the mouth speaks."[8] I think it's equally safe to say, "Out of the abundance of the heart, the comment section speaks."

People were not outraged that babies were representing themselves in court, thus increasing their chances of deportation to the cartel-controlled, war-torn, destitute situations they were fleeing from. They were outraged that KB sounded like a liberal! The conversation was almost exclusively political. The toxic attitudes about the life decisions of immigrants who chose to risk their lives to come to this country were on full display with comments like "I blame the parents," "America is not here to give handouts," and "Send them back."

What a horrifying commentary. Can there be any reason besides opportunity for why someone would choose to leave their home and risk their life crossing rivers and facing down thieves and wild animals to come here? I'm reminded of the words of the British poet Warsan Shire: "No one puts their children in a boat unless the water is safer than the land."[9]

The instability of Mexico is greatly caused by the cartel whose biggest client is the United States. Through our own vice, we fund the instability of a nation! So why do our hearts slam shut when innocent people try to flee the nightmare we helped create?

One user wrote, "Was KB's account hacked . . . no Christian artist or child of God should be speaking about these things on social media."

"Child of God"? Fascinating! I believe comments like these get to the core problem of the Christian witness in America, and that is that we identify far more strongly with the heart of our political party than we do with the heart of God.

IDENTITY CRISIS

I have neither the interest nor the qualifications to propose a solution to our current policies around border security, citizenship, and the economy, but I do have an observation. Typically the first question people ask in matters of justice is "What should we do?" But it seems to me, there are two other wildly important questions that need to come first.

I believe that what we should do is predicated on first understanding "Who is God?" The Bible starts in Genesis 1:1, "In the beginning God . . . " So, too, should we start all of our conversations about justice. Until we get that right, we are lost to understand the next question, which is, "Who should we be?" Why these two questions? I am convinced that many of us are confused as to what we should do because we don't know what type of people we should be and because we don't know what type of God we serve.

Let me be clear. If the God we serve does not have an overwhelming interest in and commitment to the immigrant, the orphan, the widow, and the needy, we are not serving the God of the Bible. And can we honestly say we know God as we ought

> **IF THE GOD WE SERVE DOES NOT HAVE AN OVERWHELMING INTEREST IN AND COMMITMENT TO THE IMMIGRANT, THE ORPHAN, THE WIDOW, AND THE NEEDY, WE ARE NOT SERVING THE GOD OF THE BIBLE.**

when there are places that are overflowing with immigrants, orphans, and widows, yet many of us look at them and not only feel nothing and do nothing but also attack the people who are trying to do something? What could be more unlike God? Who do we think we are?

When people ask me what I do for a living, sometimes I freeze. Although I'm an author, a business owner, and a Christian teacher, I am mainly known for rapping. The problem is, when I tell people I'm a rapper, they think that is synonymous with not having a job. So I normally just say, "I'm an artist." But then they ask, "What kind of painting do you do?" Now I have to clarify even more, and it starts to sound like I don't have a job again! How we identify ourselves is important to us because it tells about who we are.

Well, in the book of Deuteronomy, we get a front-row seat to God identifying Himself to His newly formed people, Israel. And lest we forget, the audience for a significant portion of the Pentateuch is a recently rescued group of slaves learning about the living God for the first time. Note His intro:

> The LORD your God is the God of gods and Lord of lords, the great, mighty, and awe-inspiring God, showing no partiality and taking no bribe. He executes justice for the fatherless and the widow, and loves the resident alien, giving him food and clothing. You are also to love the resident alien, since you were resident aliens in the land of Egypt. You are to fear the LORD your God and worship him.[10]

It is clear that the Lord is especially attentive to the needs of the marginalized. It would seem, then, to be the very nature of justice for humans to have an equally prioritized concern.

Jesus opens His ministry in a similar fashion, identifying the target of His gospel: "The Spirit of the Lord is on me, because he has anointed me to preach good news to *the poor.*"[11]

Of course, this doesn't mean that God doesn't care about you if you are *not* poor. Spiritual poverty is everyone's reality. But as Tim Keller points out in his excellent book *Generous Justice*, God never identifies Himself as "the defender of the rich" and powerful, but He is constantly volunteering Himself as He who loves the immigrant, sustains the fatherless, provides justice for the needy, and demands we defend the oppressed.[12]

By the way, I love how God refers to himself as "God of gods" because He squares His personality on the backdrop of the gods the people were accustomed to. When the gods of the ancient Near East revealed themselves to the elites, the powerful treated the vulnerable as expendable. But the God of Israel says, "There is none like me: I am the God of the weak, the forgotten, the small, and the slave, and I execute justice for them all!"

Perhaps this is a good place to suggest to you a simple definition of what the Bible means by justice. Justice, put simply, is what God thinks is right. There's more to be said here, but it's essential we understand that God's heart is obsessed with what is just and in executing that justice for those who are powerless. The Scriptures say that righteousness and justice are the foundation of His throne![13]

That is who God is. Now we can start to unfurl the question, "Who should we be?"

One of my favorite verses in all of Scripture is the simple yet profound words of the prophet Micah: "Mankind, he has told each of you what is good and what it is the LORD requires of you: to act justly, to love faithfulness, and to walk humbly with your God."[14] In other words, God requires us to be with one another the way He is with us.

If God loves the immigrant, *we* must love the immigrant. There should be no Christian movement that is ostensibly hostile toward immigrants. That is the dangerous Christianity of the Land. The good-dangerous Christianity of Christ advocates for the immigrant.

If God loves the fatherless, *we* must love the fatherless. There should be no Christian movement that is interested in the fatherlessness of a community only to argue that all of their problems are their fault. That is the dangerous Christianity of the Land. The dangerous Christianity of Christ isn't looking to debate fatherlessness but to be fathers to the fatherless because that is who their God is!

If God loves the poor, *we* must love the poor. There should be no Christian movement that funnels its resources to its own brand and partnerships with the rich and the powerful. That is the dangerous Christianity of the Land. The dangerous Christianity of Christ is a burden lifter to the vulnerable among us. Beth Moore said it best: "When the gospel has become bad news to the poor, to the oppressed, to the broken-hearted and imprisoned and good news to the proud, self-righteous and privileged instead, it is no longer the gospel of our Lord Jesus Christ."[15]

We discussed before how Matthew 25 explains the basis for which Jesus separates the redeemed from the lost, the "sheep" from the "goats." Interestingly enough, the redeemed and the lost were both judged by how they did justice for the poor, the hungry, the sick, and the naked—"the least of these." What is particularly profound about Jesus' explanation, however, is that He refers to these poor, naked, hungry, sick, and incarcerated people as His "brothers." Rejecting "the least of these" is rejecting Jesus Himself.

Given that, can we say we know a God who is drawn to the least of these when we are only drawn to the least inconvenient? If we don't have an answer for who the least of these are among us now, we probably won't have an answer on Judgment Day.

Brothers and sisters, the justice of the Christianity of Christ is not a side issue or a matter of charity; it's a matter of eternity. Job, one of the Bible's most pristine portraits of righteousness, said that if he failed to care for the vulnerable around him, "let my arm be broken from its socket."[16]

Faith in Christ Jesus alone is what saves a soul, but faith looks like something. It has fruit that confirms the identity of the root. In other words, it looks like *justice*. Our "acting justly" doesn't earn us right standing, but it does confirm that we are standing rightly.

Justice and mercy are often segregated in the Christianity of the Land, but in Scripture, they are attached at the hip.

We are talking about how Scripture defines social justice. The phrase has been hijacked, stuffed with all kinds of definitions, and then deployed as a buzzword for a new culture war. But when the translators for the English Standard Version of the Bible used the phrase as the heading for Exodus 22 in 2001, or when St. Basil the Great wrote "On Social Justice" in the fourth century, they meant what I mean: doing what God thinks is right in the society.

I love the way John Wesley described social justice. He called it "social holiness," connecting just acts toward others to holy living. As the author of Hebrews says, "Without [holiness] no one will see the Lord."[17] This helps us feel the weight of what we are talking about.

JUST MERCY

Many of us are familiar with the memoir turned box office smash *Just Mercy*, which tells the story of defense attorney Bryan Stevenson fighting for the freedom of the falsely convicted Walter McMillian. Stevenson, a Harvard Law graduate, intentionally stations himself in Alabama for the purpose of defending the defenseless, and that's exactly what he has done for dozens of falsely accused, rescuing some from the very jaws of the death penalty itself!

In an interview with *The Christian Post*, Stevenson revealed the guiding principle for his life's work: "My faith influences and shapes everything I do. . . . I remember growing up and the preacher would read from the prophet Micah: 'What does the Lord require of you? To act justly, and to love mercy and to walk humbly with God.'"[18]

Mercy is typically defined as choosing compassion when harm is within your right or power. It is often perceived as optional and seen as much more closely related to charity than justice. But for Stevenson and many lawyers who work pro bono on behalf of the vulnerable, their efforts are not acts of charity but obligation, meaning that to not act in mercy on behalf of the underrepresented would be a failure to do the right thing—a failure of justice. This is very closely related to how Scripture defines justice. Justice and mercy are often segregated in the Christianity of the Land, but in Scripture, they are attached at the hip. Consider the following verses:

Woe to you, scribes and Pharisees, hypocrites! . . . You have neglected the more important matters of the law—justice, mercy, faithfulness.[19]

Gracious is the LORD, and righteous [just];
    our God is merciful.[20]

Great is your mercy, O LORD,
    give me life according to your rules [justice].[21]

The LORD is waiting to show you mercy,
and is rising up to show you compassion,
for the LORD is a just God.
All who wait patiently for him are happy.[22]

Why is mercy so connected to justice? Because the lack of mercy toward those around us is unjust, and lack of justice leads to mercilessness! Justice is doing what is right. Mercy is taking what is right to those who need it most, even when those who need it don't necessarily deserve it. This is how the gospel of Jesus works: "While we were still sinners, Christ died for us."[23] Mercy was His disposition, and the death of Christ was God's call for justice for my law breaking. The gospel is just mercy. If that sounds strange to you, it might be helpful to further explore how justice is laid out for us in the Scriptures.

Justice in Scripture is typically displayed in two dimensions. It's first about punishing wrong—"You do the crime, you do the time." You know, *Law and Order* vibes. But it is also presented as giving people what is right.

Everyone made in the image of God has value that demands certain inalienable rights that are never to be violated. You are not to be harmed unjustly. You are not to be oppressed. You are not to be enslaved. You are not to be forbidden food. You are not to be forgotten. We are not merely doing favors for folks when we honor their rights. We are doing what is required of us.

Mercy in the First Testament is often translated from the beautiful Hebrew word *hesed*—a covenant-level grace and compassion. When Micah says to "love mercy," he is calling us to love to be gracious, to love to be compassionate, to love to be long-suffering, recognizing that we are *commanded* to do it because left to our own selfish, short-fused, graceless hearts, we would not.

"I CAN'T BREATHE"

When George Floyd was brutally murdered, the world erupted with cries for justice and mercy for the people of African descent living all over the world. Many of us cried our eyes out watching a grown man pleading for his life, saying, "I can't breathe," and crying out for his deceased mother as he teetered in and out of consciousness. We cried because George Floyd is made in the image of God, and an assault on the image of God is indeed an assault on God Himself. We cried because many of us saw ourselves, our children, and our parents in the eyes of George Floyd, because almost every Black person we knew had been a victim of some level of an officer's abuse of power. We cried because though we march, protest, and organize, this present evil persists, obstructing the progress that God's image bearers are owed.

What was disheartening was watching the army of people who profess Christ joining the defense of the officer (who, incidentally, had choked another young Black man several years prior) while simultaneously demonizing George Floyd. Talks of Floyd's criminal record, what he was doing before he was arrested, and his preexisting conditions (as if something in his blood work might explain why a handcuffed man needed a knee on his neck for ten minutes) became the playbook. And it wasn't the first time.

When Breonna Taylor was shot in her own home as the result of a botched police investigation, folks pointed out that she wasn't married to her boyfriend and therefore was living in sin.

When Ahmaud Arbery was shot down by neighborhood vigilantes, folks argued he wasn't jogging but scoping out a potential robbery. (All of his victimizers were later found guilty.)

When Botham Jean was shot by an off-duty officer who accidentally broke into his apartment, folks pointed out there was a little bit of marijuana in the house.

In every case, there was a concerted effort to erase the need to care, advocate, or mourn. Compassion, it seems, is reserved only for perfect victims. I'm reminded of Jesus' parable about the Good Samaritan who ministered to the needs of a man who had been beaten, robbed, and left for dead. Let us not blow past the fact that this parable shows an unbelieving Samaritan—or at least, not a member of the audience's household of faith—who did something about the man in need.

I don't know what the alleged "men of God" who skipped past their neighbor's suffering were thinking, but if they were anything like us, I wonder if they thought:

- *He's probably got alcohol in his system.*
- *He knew robbers are around at night. Why was he out so late?*
- *He probably robbed those men. They were just defending themselves.*

The Samaritan didn't need all the facts. He simply cared (mercy) and did the right thing in helping (justice). Jesus underwrites the Samaritan's behavior as an example of what it means to follow God in loving our neighbor.

Would there be a need for the sentiment "Black Lives Matter" if our faith communities already communicated that? Black Lives Matter as an organization is rife with ideas and practices I would not endorse; nevertheless, they have led the conversation on justice in part because too many Christians have not.

The Christianity of the Land obsesses over the efficiency of its opponents' proposed solutions without itself having an efficient alternative. Instead of protesting the injustice, we protest the protest. Instead of proposing a solution, we critique the critique. When we label everyone trying to bring the Kingdom of God to bear on injustice Marxists and liberals, we punt the conversation to actual Marxists and liberals. If BLM, LGBTQ+, and Marxists have a better sense of protecting the lives of the vulnerable and understand grace enough to see the vulnerable past their sins, is that not an indictment of us? Do they have a better understanding of the heart of God than we do?

Meanwhile, churches are almost as segregated on racial lines in Sunday morning worship services as they were during the legal segregation of the1960s.[24] The *New York Times* covered the "quiet exodus" of Black worshipers from white Christian spaces,[25] yet it is those who identify as Christian who are often more likely to maintain that race is not a big issue in our country.

"WHAT DOES THE LORD REQUIRE OF YOU?"

There are indeed multiple communities in our country who are not valued as they should be, not seen as they should be, and who are falling through the cracks. They do not have the favor of this world, but they are loved by God. What would happen if the dangerous Christianity of Christ was alive in us and aimed at these people, armed with justice and mercy, never forgetting that the core of our fight for justice is the promise of God that He will make all things new for those who believe?

Doing just mercy commands the full scope of the gospel, whose chief effect is rescuing and reuniting people with their Creator. All of our efforts adorn, point to, and capitalize the ultimate, eternal act of just mercy, Christ's death on the cross. God graciously sent His Son to rescue those oppressed by Satan, sin, and death, to rescue them from spiritual, mental, and subsequent social poverty and from their own fear, guilt, and shame.

Doing justice without the gospel is not just a failure of justice; it is a cruel and unloving thing to do. Doing evangelism without just mercy is faith without works. It is unbiblical, unholy, and without love. It is a message that lacks credibility with the people we want to reach. It postures our work so as to be ignored. We need the whole gospel. We need to go do justice.

DOING EVANGELISM WITHOUT JUST MERCY IS FAITH WITHOUT WORKS. IT IS UNBIBLICAL, UNHOLY, AND WITHOUT LOVE.

Identify the "least of these" among you. This is not a call to find some minorities. Minority doesn't mean outside of power. This is a call to identify anyone in your orbit that is hurting, overlooked, and underserved—widows, orphans, the elderly, immigrants, the impoverished. Make a list and pray to God to give you an opportunity to serve them. Then go do justice.

Pray daily for God to keep you merciful toward others as He has been merciful toward you. Argue less with antisocial justice trolls. Go do justice.

Do not be afraid to hear the observations of people outside the faith community (Samaritans) on how society is failing its vulnerable people. Respect the image of God enough to believe victims can honestly share their victimization without knowing Jesus. Go do justice.

There will inevitably be places where you agree with BLM, critical race theorists, and even socialists. Do not fear that your faith is now in jeopardy because someone you perceive as an ideological opponent has a good (or better) point. All truth is God's truth, and it will be in these truth intersections that we find windows to proclaim the excellency of Christ!

CHAPTER 6

DANGEROUS LOVE

Call me every name under the sun but you won't get rise, I am not the one.
"I AM NOT THE ONE"

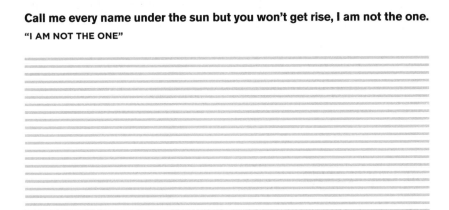

I've been traveling the world for over a decade, rapping, singing, teaching, and preaching Jesus on every stage imaginable—from the Rikers Island correctional facility and the Dallas Cowboys' AT&T Stadium to public schools in Sydney, Australia, and the cold streets of West Philly. From outreaches, conferences, services, protests, tours, appearances, and think tanks, I have been part of more expressions of Christian ministry than I can even remember. As a consequence, I've met just about every contemporary Christian influencer or leader imaginable, and as I think about the profiles of all the great Christian influencers in our world, there are always at least two traits that really explain their draw: they are gifted speakers, and they are popular. And when those two traits are accompanied by charisma, good looks, and partnership with other gifted, charismatic, good-looking people, it's a recipe for Christian-culture greatness.

Although there is nothing inherently wrong with any of these traits, who we elevate says a lot about what we value. And what we value says a lot about who we are. The Christianity of the Land would have us organize the giants of faith according to people's love for a person, but the Christianity of Christ identifies the giants of faith according to a person's love for people. That might explain why year after year we watch "great men of God" nosedive their ministries, marriages, and the reputation of the Lord Jesus right into the ground, reminding us that the size of someone's giftedness and platform has zero correlation to the size of their faith.

It is not giftedness or popularity that is truly impressive in the Christianity of Christ—it is only love. There's an old boxing adage that says, "Hard work beats talent when talent doesn't work hard." Well, I submit to you that love also beats talent when talent lacks love!

THE LAW OF LAWS

Christ Jesus, the supreme embodiment of all that is righteous, truthful, and beautiful in the world, has a law. His law is the zenith of all of God's moral codes. Indeed, His law is the law that every moral code under the sun testifies to. I call it the "law of laws." And Paul says that the way we live out the "law of laws" is by helping to carry the burden or lighten the suffering of the people around us.[1] This willingness to bear someone else's burdens, this willingness to "lay down our lives for our friends,"[2] is the very essence of Christian love.

We've all heard the summary of the Christian life based on what Jesus said is the greatest commandment: "Love God and your neighbor." I've repeated it many times for many years. I've even merchandised the phrase on a tee. But very recently, I reread the actual verse and was shocked to realize I have been doing a disservice to the full meaning of the text for years. Like the childhood game of telephone, if we are not taking what we are repeating back to the source, it is destined for convolution.

In Mathew 22, Jesus is being pressed by religious leaders to produce the single greatest commandment God has revealed to His people. Here's what Jesus actually says: "You shall love the Lord your God with all your heart and with all your soul and with all your mind. This is the great and first commandment. And a second is like it: You shall love your neighbor as yourself. On these two commandments depend all the Law and the Prophets."[3]

Jesus gives them not one but *two* commandments: love God with everything you've got, and love other people the way you love yourself. But verse 39 makes it clear that Jesus is still only giving one answer. When Jesus says, "A second is like it," He is basically saying, "What I am about to say is inextricably connected to the thing I just said." Stated even more plainly, the two commandments are so dependent on each other that if you were to separate loving God from loving neighbor, as far as God is concerned, you would be doing neither. Still, we do not want to lose the distinction and the order of the two components of the great commandment because conforming our hearts, souls, and minds to loving and following God is what makes neighbor love possible.

But, brothers and sisters, please do not miss the point that one of the primary ways in which God is worshiped, loved, and served is through our loving others the way we love ourselves.

ONE OF THE PRIMARY WAYS IN WHICH GOD IS WORSHIPED, LOVED, AND SERVED IS THROUGH OUR LOVING OTHERS THE WAY WE LOVE OURSELVES.

It's easy to take comfort in the dimensions of faith that are virtually invisible. Private devotion, prayer, reading, contemplation, and discussions about truth are essential, but those things alone are not the indicators of a life that "walk[s] in love."[4] This is why the second component of the great commandment is just as important as the first. The strength of our obedience to the first commandment is fully realized in our demonstration of the second. In other words, if anyone thinks he has understood God or Scripture but cannot build up, as Augustine calls it, "double love" for God and neighbor, he has not understood anything at all. Our devotion to God isn't completed in our piety but in our demonstrable acts of care for others. The apostle John picks up on this theme when he says, "Let us not love in word or speech, but in action and in truth."[5]

This point is so important that it comes up again in Luke 10, when a young lawyer asks Jesus, "What must I do to inherit eternal life?" Jesus responds, "What is written in the law?" In other words, "What does the Bible say?" And the lawyer says, "'Love the Lord your God with all your heart, with all your soul, with all your strength, and with all your mind,' and 'your neighbor as yourself.'"[6]

Note the context of the lawyer's question is "How do I get eternal life?" which tells us that there is indeed a high price for failing to obey the "law of laws." But I'd like to draw your attention to where Jesus shifts the conversation to the lawyer's second question. The Scripture says, "Wanting to justify himself, he asked Jesus, 'And who is my neighbor?'"[7] I find that so fascinating. Here we have this lawyer staring into the eyes of the Son of God, not flinching at all over the first component of the great commandment, yet still needing clarification on the second half. He's like, "Love God with everything? Check! But who is the other person You want me to love?" It's almost as if the lawyer takes cover under the internal and often invisible professions of love for God in which He is the main witness but is shaky on the part of love for God that is visible and demonstrable, held accountable by the people he is called to serve.

Jesus, of course, masterfully responds with His famous story of the Good Samaritan:

A man was going down from Jerusalem to Jericho and fell into the hands of robbers. They stripped him, beat him up, and fled, leaving him half dead. A priest happened to be going down that road. When he saw him, he passed by on the other side. In the same way, a Levite, when he arrived at the place and saw him, passed by on the other side. But a Samaritan on his journey came up to him, and when he saw the man, he had compassion. He went over to him and bandaged his wounds, pouring on olive oil and wine. Then he put him on his own animal, brought him to an inn, and took care of him. The next day he took out two denarii, gave them to the innkeeper, and said, "Take care of him. When I come back I'll reimburse you for whatever extra you spend."

"Which of these three do you think proved to be a neighbor to the man who fell into the hands of the robbers?"

"The one who showed mercy to him," [the lawyer] said.

Then Jesus told him, "Go and do the same."[8]

Jesus is saying here that we shouldn't worry about who our neighbors are so we can draw circles around who we don't have to care about. Instead, we are to concern ourselves with *being* loving neighbors to whoever around us is in need. *That* is loving God.

I was once on tour with a prominent Christian artist who had recently decided to use his platform to support the "anti-woke" movement, a counterprotest to Black Lives Matter and the social justice movement. Having toured with this brother before, I noticed a harshness and, respectfully, a dismissiveness in his rhetoric that I had not heard from him before. Believing in the sincerity of this brother's heart, I pulled him aside to express a few of my concerns. Though I thought he had plenty of good things to say and many of his critiques were indeed valid, I feared he might be, to use Jesus' phrase, straining the gnat but swallowing the camel—straining the gnat of how precisely we talk about justice while swallowing the camel of injustice itself. I shared with him studies like the *American Journal of Public Health* study that showed that Black women are 3.5 times more likely to die in child delivery than their non-Black counterparts.[9] I tried to appeal to all the stories of sisters from my church being ignored in hospitals—in several cases, to death. I wanted him to feel the shock of the peer-reviewed study published in 2020 in the *Proceedings of the National Academy of Sciences* that found that Black babies are less likely to survive infancy if their doctor is not Black.[10] I asked him, "What would you do if your friend told you this?"

He responded with a story about how back in the '90s there was a big emphasis on "saving the whales" in the music industry, and though the situation with whales was bad, it didn't need to be his concern. Setting aside how wildly offensive it is to compare whales to women, my brother's response was essentially "Why do I have to care?"

Or better, "Who is my neighbor?"

This is not to say that we can (or should) fight all the battles of the present evil age. But we have a unique obligation to fight the battles of our neighbors, those around us. We do for our neighbors what we wish we could do for the world.

"THE GREATEST OF THESE . . ."

Brothers and sisters, who are the greatest theologians among us? Who are the greatest examples of faith and godliness? Are they the gifted articulators of deep theological truths? Are they the well-followed, celebrity-recognized pastors and preachers? For my charismatic brothers and sisters, is the prophet or prophetess who seems to know your private sins or who can accurately tell you some fact about yourself before they predict your future the greatest theologian? No. The greatest theologians, preachers, pastors, or Christians among us are those that love greatly, because we are never more in love with God than when we are loving the people He created.

The Christianity of the Land would have us believe that things like platform, power, and popularity are tantamount to piety, but that is wrong. In fact, it's worse—it is *dangerous.* The Christianity of Christ is an others-loving religion. It does not place self at the center of its existence but seriously considers how it might leverage its power, resources, and life to empower those around it.

WE ARE NEVER MORE IN LOVE WITH GOD THAN WHEN WE ARE LOVING THE PEOPLE HE CREATED.

There is an amazing scene in C. S. Lewis's *The Great Divorce* where the narrator sees a beautiful woman being honored in a magnificent parade in heaven. There are musicians, people are throwing flowers at her feet, and she is surrounded by children and animals. Assuming she is someone of great importance, the narrator asks his guide who she is, and his guide tells him, "It's someone ye'll never have heard of." He explains to him that all of the young people surrounding her, though not her own children, are still counted as her sons and daughters, as "every young man or boy that met her became her son—even if it was only the boy that brought the meat to her back door. Every girl that met her was her daughter." Likewise, he tells him, "Every beast and bird that came near her had its place in her love. . . . And now the abundance of life she has in Christ from the Father flows over into them."[11]

We've so often got it backwards, thinking that the greatest Christians must be the ones who command the biggest spotlight. But this is a powerful reminder that "fame in [heaven] and fame on Earth are two quite different things,"[12] and love is the measure of the greater fame. Brothers and sisters, do not mistake "likes" for love. It's not popularity that marks nearness to God.

But to be clear, nearness to God is also not about hyper humility and separatism. Praying and reading your Bible for eight hours a day might be commendable pursuits, but solitary devotion—in and of itself—is not the height of spirituality. I hope I'm sounding like a broken record: loving other people, helping those in need, and sacrificing—giving of yourself to others—draws us closer to God.

As Paul said in his letter to the Corinthians,

If I speak in the tongues of men and of angels, but have
not love, I am a noisy gong or a clanging cymbal. And
if I have prophetic powers, and understand all mysteries
and all knowledge, and if I have all faith, so as to remove
mountains, but have not love, I am nothing. If I give away
all I have, and if I deliver up my body to be burned, but
have not love, I gain nothing.[13]

There was a situation a few years ago that put my love for others
to the test.

I like only one sport—boxing—and my favorite boxer in the
whole world is a fighter named Andre Ward. Andre is an Olympic
gold medalist who retired undefeated, and he was (still is) my
lowercase-*i* idol. He asked me to join him on his ring walk for a big
fight he had coming up, performing a song, which held the same
value as Bill Gates calling to say he had a billion dollars for me.

Well, it turned out that the day of the fight I was scheduled to
give a concert for a small youth group in some obscure town. Now,
I could have easily canceled the show. It wouldn't have affected my
career at all, and whatever money I would have lost I would have
made back ten times over by walking Andre Ward to the ring!

But I knew that the God-honoring thing to do in that situation
was to keep my commitment. It was a hard decision to make, but I
just knew it was the right thing to do. So instead of walking Andre
Ward to the ring and performing on a Pay-Per-View event that would
have been seen by millions, I spent the day in some obscure town
doing a concert for three hundred youth group kids, and I had to
watch the fight on my phone. And you know . . . it burned. But it
was a situation where I had to decide: *Am I gonna choose what's right,
or am I gonna choose what serves me?*

I'm not telling this story to flex. I even called that youth group to see if there was any way they would work with me and change the date. That's how badly I wanted to walk Andre to the ring! So it wasn't like the decision was automatic. I just share this story as an example of what we are all called to do—to put our love for others ahead of our love for ourselves.

THERE'S NO "I" IN LOVE

The Christianity of the Land is the product of the values of the culture, and I can think of few American values more incompatible with the Christianity of Christ than individualism. We are deathly committed to our own interest, our own family, our own stuff, and any call to "share what's mine" sounds like an indictment of the American dream—because it is! But it is particularly fascinating that the majority of New Testament authors addressed their writings not to individuals but to churches.

Because we typically perceive the goal of the Bible to be making Jesus our personal Lord and Savior, the assumption is that the Bible is written just to "me." But it's not. It's written to communities. In his letter to the Ephesians, Paul writes,

> So, then, you are no longer foreigners and strangers, but
> fellow citizens with the saints, and members of God's
> household, built on the foundation of the apostles and
> prophets, with Christ Jesus himself as the cornerstone. In
> him the whole building, being put together, grows into a
> holy temple in the Lord. In him you are also *being built
> together* for God's dwelling in the Spirit.[14]

This is a hard obstacle for Western culture to overcome. Don't get me wrong—the Bible obviously cares about the individual. But the Bible also calls us to be part of the body of Christ, and as Paul writes in his letter to the Corinthians,

God has so composed the body . . . that there may be no division in the body, but that the members may have the same care for one another. If one member suffers, all suffer together; if one member is honored, all rejoice together. Now you are the body of Christ and individually members of it.[15]

There are two powerful sisters in my community—Julie and Allison—who have had a tremendous impact on the spiritual life of my wife. Together, they have been a gospel force in the city, discipling women of all ages, races, and ethnicities in the Word of God. About three years ago, Julie entered into what must have been the most difficult season of her life. On July 22, 2019—I'll never forget the date because she and her husband were leaving my birthday party when they got the news—she was notified by the police that her only son had been killed in a hit-and-run accident. But that was not the only devastating news she received that year. Julie's doctor informed her that her ongoing fight with an autoimmune disorder had so damaged her kidneys that she would need a transplant as soon as possible.

Brothers and sisters, I am emotional as I write this because the events that followed changed me forever. The community of God rushed to love, care for, and serve Julie in ways that words cannot describe. Julie's husband, Darryl, said it felt like the very presence of God had rushed to their aid and comfort. Upon hearing of our sister's condition, Allison and several other members of the community were willing to give up their own kidneys, provided they were a match. Allison was! Prayerfully, the two sisters underwent surgery, connected by nothing more than the blood of Christ and the love they had for one another. The surgery was a success! God was glorified, the city was impacted by this high-definition display of Christ's love, and the church was strengthened.

This is the good-dangerous, world-altering, culture-impacting love of the Christianity of Christ. We will not all be called to lay down our lives (or our organs), but we *are* all called to arm ourselves with a mindset that is willing to give freely of ourselves for the cause of love.

IT'S THE THOUGHT THAT COUNTS

There is a popular saying when it comes to doing good for others that "it's the thought that counts." For example, let's say you decide to do something nice for a coworker, so you bring them a pint of ice cream. But then you find out they're lactose intolerant. They'll usually respond, "That's okay. It's the thought that counts." What they're really saying, though, is not "how nice that you *thought* of it" but "how nice that you actually *did* something for me." Just thinking of something doesn't necessarily show love. I mean, it's nice, but love is in the doing. How else are we supposed to know you thought of doing something if you don't actually do it—you know what I'm saying?

Jesus' brother, James the Just, writes,

> What good is it, my brothers, if someone says he has faith but does not have works? Can that faith save him? If a brother or sister is poorly clothed and lacking in daily food, and one of you says to them, "Go in peace, be warmed and filled," without giving them the things needed for the body, what good is that? So also faith by itself, if it does not have works, is dead.[16]

To quote bestselling author Bob Goff, "love does." But there's more to it than that.

There was a popular TV show back in the early 2000s called *Pimp My Ride.* It was hosted by the rapper Xzibit, and they would find people who were struggling financially and driving hoopdies or old cars, and one day Xzibit would just show up at their house and say, "I got good news for you. I'm gonna pimp your ride." The person would usually explode in excitement and hand the keys over to Xzibit. A few weeks later, he would come back with this outrageously customized, over-the-top ride with a hot tub in the trunk or a TV roof or a flame thrower for exhaust pipes.

The thing is, these upgrades looked incredibly cool, but they were also incredibly impractical and sometimes dangerous. In fact, the show faced tremendous ridicule when it came out that they were making ridiculous renovations that looked great on TV but that rendered the car undrivable, caused it to break down, or required so much maintenance that the owners couldn't afford it anymore. I mean, as awesome as it might be to have a fifty-inch TV in your car, ain't no insurance company touching that. And I can't imagine much—if any—of that stuff was covered under warranty. I'm certain manufacturers were like, "Whose idea was it to put a fireplace in a Chevy in the first place?"

The point is, even though it *looked* like they were helping these (literally) poor people, they really weren't. They weren't thinking about what would genuinely be helpful—like, say, a clean, safe car that actually ran, an offer to pay the car off, or a year's worth of free gas. They were just thinking, *What would be good for ratings?* It was all about appearances. Plenty of flash but no substance. And once they dropped the car back off, that was it—they were gone. One and done. How easy is it to still center ourselves in our acts of love instead of the needs of the ones we are aiming to impact?

I'm reminded of the time I bought a $6,000 ring for my wife for our five-year anniversary—a hefty upgrade from the $600 ring I married her with. I remember sitting her down and presenting the ring, slowly unveiling the largest purchase of my life, confident I would earn enough brownie points to last me for years. Instead, I was met with a look of disappointment.

"Wait, you don't like it?" I awkwardly asked.

"No," she said, "I love it. But you have to take it back."

There are zero exceptions to Christ's command to love your neighbor.

I thought, *She has to be joking.* "Why?"

She looked at me and said, "We are about to have a baby, and we are in the middle of buying a house. It would be irresponsible to keep this ring."

Shocked as I was, because Michelle does the finances in our house, I knew she was right. But what really struck me is what she said next.

"I appreciate the thought," she said, "I really do, but what truly brings me joy and makes me feel loved is when you don't throw your dirty clothes all over the floor but put them in the hamper. It's not the big stuff but all the little things that make me feel seen, heard, and loved."

Saving $6K was music to my frugal ears, but more important was the lesson about what it means to really love others. It's not always the big things—like souped-up cars or fancy rings—that make the difference. It's the acts that truly have the other person's interests at the center, even if it's as simple as doing the laundry or filling a tank with gas. These small acts of love may not serve our Instagram feeds well, but they serve the Kingdom and lift those who are around us.

ONE STEP FURTHER

Jesus said to His disciples, "Love one another: just as I have loved you, you also are to love one another. By this all people will know that you are my disciples, if you have love for one another."[17] Likewise, He instructed His disciples to "love your neighbor as yourself" and to "love your enemies, do what is good to those who hate you, bless those who curse you, pray for those who mistreat you."[18]

Brothers and sisters, there are zero exceptions to Christ's command to love your neighbor. No religious exceptions. No political exceptions. No sexuality exceptions. No ethnic exceptions. There isn't even an enemy exception!

Enemy is a pretty strong word. Most people tend to think along extreme lines, like terrorists, or they think along petty lines, like those we merely disagree with. But I think the more general application of what Jesus is talking about is anyone who stands in intentional opposition to your well-being.

No matter who our enemies are or how they have hurt or offended us, we are commanded to love them—full stop. That does not mean to excuse them or exist as a punching bag for all their assaults. But it does mean that we should posture ourselves for reconciliation, pray for their well-being, and not refuse them help if the opportunity arises. That is a major focus—an epicenter— of the Christianity of Christ.

This is hard. Not because it's too complicated but precisely because it is not. We have nowhere to run and no room to evade the obvious and straightforward command of Jesus. But there is so much reward in obedience.

The mechanics of Jesus' love are that hate doesn't drive out hate. When people are being graceless toward us, adding more graceless-ness to the conversation may feel satisfying to the flesh, but it's det-rimental to the soul and the situation. A friend of mine always says, "We are all broken. Broken things have sharp edges, so when we get close to each other, we cut."

We think in terms of enemies when we start sharpening our edges so we can stab other people with them. There is only one alternative that paves the path to redemption, and that is the utter rejection of hate. And that starts by remembering that the people who oppose us are, first and foremost, *people*.

In his book *The Pursuit of Holiness*, Jerry Bridges tells a story about a preacher that was seated next to a drunk man on a train. Each time the man took a drink, he offered some to the preacher, but the preacher politely turned him down. Embarrassed, the drunk man eventually said, "You must think I'm a pretty rough guy." To which the preacher responded, "Not at all. I think you're a very generous-hearted fellow."[19]

The first step in loving our enemies is to not reduce them to the thing we think they're wrong about but instead to appreciate the complexity of who they are. Brothers and sisters, we are all sinners, but as 1 John 4:19 tells us, "We love because he first loved us." And love, as Peter reminds us, "covers a multitude of sins."[20]

We can't allow transgender individuals to be beaten in the streets because of where they've landed regarding their gender. We cannot allow the abuse of an image bearer because they've made decisions that we unanimously would not endorse. In Ephesians, Paul reminds the church that they are to be "speaking the truth in love,"[21] a principle that certainly extends to our interactions with the world. Given that the word "love" in this verse translates the Greek *agape*—self-sacrificial love that insists on the benefit of the loved one—perhaps this is better translated as "speak the truth *out of* love." This is a call not merely to tell people the truth politely but to speak the truth as a person whose actions demonstrate they love the person they are talking to. Telling the truth is loving, but if the only time we love people we disagree with is when we are telling them they are wrong, are we really speaking the truth in love?

Loving our ideological enemies might mean advocating for them—not because we agree with their conclusions, but because, like us, they are loved by God.

DON'T BE A DOORMAT

When delivering His Sermon on the Mount, Jesus told His followers,

> Don't resist an evildoer. On the contrary, if anyone slaps you on your right cheek, turn the other to him also. As for the one who wants to sue you and take away your shirt, let him have your coat as well. And if anyone forces you to go one mile, go with him two. Give to the one who asks you, and don't turn away from the one who wants to borrow from you.[22]

Let's be clear. Jesus' commands to "bless and do not curse" and to "turn the other cheek" are not calls to enable abusers. Jesus is not telling us to become the doormats for all humanity. Love is not centered on self, but it certainly includes it—we are to love our neighbors *as we love ourselves*. We are to love the image of God in our own bodies enough to defend it. Turning the other cheek is not a call to pacifism. Jesus, quite literally, didn't turn the other cheek when he was slapped before the high priest. Jesus is giving us a picture of how the children of God deal with the insults of this world. Jesus is saying that we should be so buried in Kingdom reality that we defy the insults of this world to the point that they become occasions to love! This is an unshakable place to be. The ultimate flex is to respond to insults with blessing. As Peter writes, "Be compassionate and humble, not paying back evil for evil or insult for insult but, on the contrary, giving a blessing, since you were called for this, so that you may inherit a blessing."[23]

Shortly after I became a believer, I was at a youth group event at the church I was attending, and there was this dude that would show up every once in a while to try and get with the girls. He wasn't a Christian, mind you; he was just trying to shoot his shot. And he knew there would always be a lot of young, impressionable girls hanging out at the youth group gatherings.

Anyway, on this particular night, he showed up and started taunting me. I don't know why. I must have done something to set him off—looked at him the wrong way or something. It didn't take much. This dude loved to fight, and everybody on the south side of St. Petersburg knew it. Nobody ever wanted to play basketball with him because every time he stepped on the court, there'd be some kind of altercation that he was happy to instigate. He didn't even really have "hands," as a boxer might say, but that didn't stop him from throwing blows at every opportunity.

We started off sitting on opposite sides of the room, but he kept moving closer and closer. Then, once I was in earshot, he started calling me weak and saying all kinds of other stuff that I don't care to repeat. I just laughed it off, smiled at him, and said, "God bless you, brother." You would have thought I said something about his mother because he got so angry, he threw a bunch of chairs out of the way and stepped to my face. I stood up immediately, and we were nose to nose. He shouted at me, "Man, I will knock you out right now!"

I simply responded, "I love you with the love of Christ."

"Oh, so you gay now?" he said.

"You can call it whatever you want, brother," I told him. "I love you with the love of Christ."

He just kept trying to get a rise out of me, and I kept saying, "I love you" and "I pray God's blessing on you."

It got awkward. There was no way for him to escalate. He stared at me for a second, said, "Okay," and walked away. If I remember correctly, he came to me later that night and shook my hand. I actually played ball with him several times after that day, and it was all love.

I know that story is a lot neater than the normal messiness of life, but it's true. When he could not overcome my love with his hate, his hate was overcome by my love.

Brothers and sisters, we are called to love—simply, purely, completely. This indeed includes the well-being of others and also those who oppose us. I have a personal commitment to seriously consider how I might do good to anyone in my community who comes to me with a need. Even if I can only pray. This is what love does.

The next time you are cursed, criticized by an anonymous troll on the Internet, or unfairly attacked, before you respond, remember, "Do not be overcome by evil, but overcome evil with good."[24] Do not allow yourself to become so blinded by the inclinations of the flesh that you miss the path of healing—the way of love. "Let all that you do be done in love."[25]

CHAPTER 7

DANGEROUS FRIENDSHIPS

I'm John Wick for my dogs.
"ANOTHER WIN"

I can't wait until the day comes when I sit down with my grand-children and tell them stories from "back in the day." I think it would be amusing if my mind is sharp enough to remember what occurred but dull enough to forget I've already shared the same story fifty times. In a sense, it would always feel fresh in my memory. I've already planned to habitually recount the craziness of the 2020 global pandemic. I'm excited to dramatize tales of vaccines and 5G tower conspiracies, Chinese labs, murder hornets, the face mask war, the terrible Australian wildfires, and global protests. I imagine myself concluding each rendering of the tale with the same adage: "Believe it or not, the truth is stranger than fiction"—or something unnecessarily deep like that.

I was actually exposed to COVID-19 in the early goings. Since I have two immunosuppressed people in my home, my quarantine was extra isolated, all tucked away in a small room in the back of the house. By God's grace, I tested negative twice—confirming I was Corona free—but it was nearly a week before it was safe for me to spatially reengage with my family. It was especially difficult because my daughter, Nala, had just been born, and all I could do was listen to her crying and cooing through the door, knowing that my wife would have to handle the new parenting duties without me. Those five days were terrible! I remember texting my wife, "Loneliness is painful."

Though my predicament was challenging, I know a lot of people had it much worse. I can only imagine what it must have felt like to contract the virus and have to spend days, weeks, or even months in quarantine. Or worse, to slip into eternity all alone in an ICU bed.

That's when it hit me. This isn't actually new. I began reflecting on conversations I'd had with people throughout the years.

Many people—even way before the pandemic—have been living in such isolation and loneliness that they fear they may slip into eternity all alone in an ICU bed. All the good and necessary calls for social distancing and self-isolation in response to the pandemic just reified that another pandemic was already here—loneliness.

Even with all our technology, social media followings, and the ability to instantly connect with humans all across the globe, people are increasingly revealing their inability to find lasting community, friendships, and meaningful relationships.

Social media has a way of facilitating cotton candy connections that masquerade as friendships, with tons of likes, LOLs, and little heart emojis, but are actually shallow, superficial, and ultimately unfulfilling. Generation Z is probably the biggest target for this phenomenon. Considering they are the first generation to enter the world with a smartphone in hand, one might assume they are more connected than any previous generation. But the research reveals otherwise. In fact, they are believed to be the loneliest generation ever. This crisis is not just troubling; it is detrimental to human health. Dr. Douglas Nemecek, chief medical officer for behavioral health at Cigna, suggests that "loneliness has the same impact on mortality as smoking 15 cigarettes a day, making it even more dangerous than obesity."[1] And this zombie-like drift into isolation is apparently on a steady incline. According to Cigna, in 2019 "three in five Americans (61 percent) report feeling lonely, compared to more than half (54 percent) in 2018."[2] And that was before the pandemic even started. Brothers and sisters, the research is clear. The vast majority of us are suffering from loneliness-induced pain.

Of course, the church has not been immune to the seclusion trend taking over the broader culture. If anything, it has mimicked the problem. Perhaps one of the most expressed areas of suffering for many of us has been the absence of deep-rooted fellowship.

I cannot overstate how spiritually risky it is to aim to be Christian by yourself. Jesus gave His followers the church! Our faith is a communal faith. While solitude can be beneficial at times (Jesus frequently went off on His own to pray), prolonged isolation is among the devil's sharpest arrows.

The book of Proverbs speaks a lot to this dynamic. Proverbs 11:14 suggests that "Where there is no guidance, a people falls, but in an abundance of counselors there is safety" (ESV). Likewise, Proverbs 27:10 says, "Don't abandon your friend or your father's friend, and don't go to your brother's house in your time of calamity; better a neighbor nearby than a brother far away." In other words, our friends should be there for us when our family can't be. In that sense, our friends become a kind of family. Solomon even elevates friendship *over* family by saying, "There is a friend who stays closer than a brother" and "a friend loves at all times,"[3] meaning a brother is blood and will be there when you need him out of obligation, but friends are there by choice and are there out of love.

The more I find references to friendship in Scripture, the more convinced I am that the fellowship of the saints is intended to be a community of friends—a collection of believers who love, celebrate, and sacrifice for each other.

The Bible uses this Greek word *koinonia* to describe what is happening between Christians doing life together. *Koinonia* means mutual bond, partner, companion, sharer of life and burdens. It's much deeper than our modern understanding of friendship, which is simply mutual affection that typically ends when someone upsets us. Koinonia is more resilient, more covenantal, more safe. And I believe the way the Bible illustrates friendship helps us truly understand what koinonia looks like, what real Christian friendship should be, and how this real Christian friendship is dangerous to the powers of darkness.

THE GOAT AND THE GARDEN

Jesus reveals the importance of Christian community in His final words before going to the cross. Knowing that His time on this earth is coming to a close, Christ chooses to spend His last moments talking about community. People's last words typically carry the weight of their legacy, and what is on Jesus' mind? His friends. Christ's prayer is that the church would "be one, as you, Father, are in me and I am in you. May they also be in us."[4] Brothers and sisters, there you have it. Jesus' last words before His brutal death are a prayer that the bond of unity that exists in the Godhead would be present in His people. The Creator of the universe exists in a friendship. From eternity, the Father, Son, and Spirit have existed together in perfect harmony, unity, and yes, friendship. Who do you think created the concept?

When we think about Christ's ministry, it's easy to overlook the centrality of friendship. Christ declares to His disciples, "I do not call you servants anymore, because a servant doesn't know what his master is doing. I have called you friends."[5] Earlier Jesus defines the greatest love as one between friends: "Greater love has no one than this, that someone lay down his life for his friends,"[6] which is precisely what Christ did on the cross. Jesus both lived and died for His friends. He is the GOAT of friendships! Someone on Twitter hilariously pointed out that Jesus' real miracle is that He had twelve friends in His thirties. Well, the miracle lives on for us today!

Not only do we see friendship revealed on the cross and in the ministry of Jesus, we also see it in the Creation narrative. God's existence in relational unity from all eternity helps explain why He felt Adam needed a companion.[7] If we are made in the image of God, then friendship is central to the very fabric of our beings. Where friendship is good, God is glorified!

Indeed, God's first problem after Creation was not sin; it was Adam's isolation. Adam needed Eve. This is not to say that God failed, initially, to meet all of Adam's needs, but rather that Adam was not postured to complete the vision of the Kingdom of God *without* Eve.

We often think of Eve as a wife, a helper, and a lover, but we don't typically think about her as Adam's friend. Happy marriages run much deeper than simply remembering your vows and not cheating on each other. Love stays in the picture, but happy marriages are more than simply keeping the covenant. We need to cherish our spouse, rejoice over their presence, long to share our world with them—that's what friends do. God saw that humanity was incomplete without relational unity because that is precisely who God is: a relationally unified Trinity. Man was created *by* friendship, *for* friendship.

MIC DROP

Our relationships within the church are designed to say something to the world around us about God. Unity is not just nice; it's necessary. In speaking of the unity of Jews and Gentiles in Jesus, groups that had formerly been at odds with each other, Paul declares, "God's multi-faceted wisdom may now be made known through the church to the rulers and authorities in the heavens."[8] The united church body exists as a witness to the cosmos that God is brilliant and like no other!

Indeed, God's design in establishing the church is a massive flex on the entire spiritual world. A united people, all in pursuit of God, is the mic drop of God's wonders in the natural and supernatural spheres. All of history has been rolling up into the presentation of the church of Jesus Christ. The church is to be the place where you find so much of God's character, so much of His will, so much of His way, and so much of His presence that its very existence declares to the world the nature and goodness of God. It is in this collection of believers—consisting of Gentiles, Jews, bound, free, rich, poor, white, black, brown, yellow—that one finds something happening that is not found anywhere else. It is a mystery how God is weaving together this grand story of all kinds of people into one body—the church, the bride of Christ. And the thread tying all of it together is the work of the Holy Spirit, demonstrated in our affection for one another. If this is true, then the church has something deeply profound to offer a lonely world. And brothers and sisters, it *is* true. The question is, will we pursue it?

The church has to be more than simply *an* answer to loneliness in our culture, because God designed the church to be *the* answer to the loneliness in our culture. In other words, people should be able to walk into our communities and find the sort of existence that heals the isolation-induced sickness that is ubiquitous throughout the world. They should be able to come to us, the gathering of God's people, and discover more than just intriguing ways to connect with other people; they should find a community *of* connected people. As Christopher Wright says in his book *The Mission of God,* "It is not so much the case that God has a mission for his church in the world but that God has a church for his mission in the world. Mission was not made for the church; the church was made for mission—God's mission."[9] The church is designed to be the space in which God accomplishes His good plan and purpose of healing, of resetting our

God designed the church to be *the* answer to the loneliness in our culture.

broken humanity, and of reconciling us to Himself. It is within the church that God radically pursues a restorative work of redeeming the image of Christ among believers, and it is through friendship with each other—modeled after the Trinity—that this good work is accomplished.

BOND OF BROTHERS

Proverbs 13:20 points out that "a companion of fools will suffer harm." Indeed, surrounding yourself with the wrong kind of people can be bad for you. As Paul writes, "Bad company ruins good morals."[10] The only thing as bad as having the wrong people around you, however, is having no one around you. Bad company ruins, and isolation suffocates.

Proverbs 18:1 states, "One who isolates himself pursues selfish desires; he rebels against all sound wisdom." All types of things seem to make perfect sense when we're alone but appear absurd when we are in the company of others.

I wrote a song years ago called "The Art of Drifting," where I tell the story of a Christian artist falling into infidelity. I wrote, "Nobody wakes up addicted. / Every great fall's from 100 bad decisions." Folks don't typically *fall* into infidelity; they *ease* into it. They back away from accountability and begin to replace the counsel of others with the counsel of me, myself, and I. And at that point, the betrayal of their Lord, spouse, and children doesn't seem so outrageous because the triune counsel of self justifies their fantasy.

It is through biblical friendship that we hold each other up, encourage each other away from stupidity, and find freedom from our sin by confessing it to each other. James encourages us, "Confess your sins to one another and pray for one another, so that you may be healed."[11]

Unhealthy isolation can fuel a guilt that falsely convicts us that we are the sum of what's wrong with us. And what is wrong with us, we then believe, is exclusive to us. We are ashamed of what we've done because of what it says about who we are. *What would happen if people knew I was a sinner?* That's terrifying to us. But consider the irrationality of isolation. PSA—we are all sinners!

That is why I submit to you that one of the essential catalysts for entering meaningful community is transparency. The *Washington Post* began touting a slogan back in 2017 about how essential it is to have a free press that can hold governments accountable. They said, "Democracy dies in darkness." It isn't just democracy that dies in darkness. *Faith* dies in the darkness, but it thrives in the light. It is not until the light of truth shines into the depths of our dysfunction that we can do anything about healing. This is why transparency is essential. When we are transparent, we say, "This is what's happening in my heart; this is exactly where I need Jesus the most."

The story of my life has been one of allowing God's people to be the hands and feet of Jesus and to minister to me in the areas where I need help. I have only shriveled under the weight of pretending I'm okay. We are not better off by getting good at running PR and image management around our brokenness. We are better off stepping into who we are—forgiven, accepted, and loved sinners whose identities are found in Jesus, not in our failures. Transparency, in part, confirms that we actually understand that reality.

I'll never forget my good friend Ameen's bachelor party the night before his wedding. A group of guys from our family and community had gathered around a firepit, and we were going around in a circle offering encouragement and advice. When my turn came, I gave an impassioned speech on the concept of intimacy in marriage as a reality that transcends sex. After finishing my little TED talk, one of the gentlemen in the circle—who we knew had more sexual exploits than the rest of us combined—stood up and said, "Whatever KB just described . . . I have *never* experienced in my life. But I want to!" He was longing for intimacy. We all do. It is no surprise to me that the only thing mainstream hip-hop artists rap about more than their various sexual exploits is the love they have for their brothers. They'll do anything for "the gang," "the guys," "the dogs." That is intimacy.

True intimacy is much deeper than sex. That is why a man can have serial sexual relationships yet remain clueless as to what it means to actually love a woman. The same principle applies to your acquaintances, which is why we can be surrounded by "friends" yet be drowning in loneliness. Intimacy is what moves us from being simply companions to having true friendship.

The Bible refers to intimacy in terms of being known, and that intimacy is crucial to what it means to be human. Toward the beginning of the story of Creation is this moment that Adam and Eve stand face-to-face in the Garden of Eden. The Scripture says that Adam "knew" his wife and that they were "naked and were not ashamed."[12] Our often pornographied minds can miss that this is a much bigger reality than sex. In fact, the Bible often uses the same language describing Adam and Eve's intimacy in strictly nonsexual contexts, most notably in reference to knowing God. A part of what it means for God to be God is His longing to be known by humanity, and what it means for humans to be human is the longing to know Him and each other. This is what we are all ultimately searching for—relationships where it's you looking into me and me looking into you, and neither of us being ashamed of what is seen. We don't need to pretend or perform; we can just *be*—fully known and fully accepted. That is true intimacy. That is true friendship. My good friend Keas Keasler coined what I think is a better term: "soul nakedness"—to be known and unashamed. That is the essence of true Christian relationships.

GOOD STUFF, BRUH

One of the best examples of intimacy in Scripture is the friendship of David and Jonathan. Following Jonathan's death, David declared, "I am distressed for you, my brother Jonathan; very pleasant have you been to me; your love to me was extraordinary, surpassing the love of women."[13]

When I first read this verse aloud in my men's group, it was met with pause because it's difficult for us to read this nowadays and not think it sounds homoerotic. But the reality is that there is not a hint of sexuality in David's relationship with Jonathan. Rather, what we do see is deep intimacy. Unfortunately, our oversexualized culture often conflates the two. Sam Alberry, in his book *7 Myths about Singleness*, explains that "In the West, we have virtually collapsed sex and intimacy into each other. We can't really conceive of genuine intimacy without its being ultimately sexual."[14] Intimacy is not synonymous with sex, and the opposite is also true. This is how David could have multiple wives and plenty of sexual activity and, like my friend at Ameen's bachelor party, not be experiencing intimacy. But through friendship, David and Jonathan were intimately connected like brothers. They had each other's back, no matter what might come. Their relationship was bound together so tightly that they would even risk their lives for each other: "Jonathan said to David, 'Whatever you say, I will do for you.'"[15] Then David "fell on his face to the ground and bowed three times. And they kissed one another and wept with one another, David weeping the most. Then Jonathan said to David, 'Go in peace, because we have sworn both of us in the name of the LORD, saying, "The LORD shall be between me and you, and between my offspring and your offspring, forever."'"[16]

Not surprisingly, men are the lonelier sex and more often suffer from a lack of intimacy. That's because it's difficult for us to connect at deep and personal levels without feeling weak—especially with other men. I remember the first time a man who wasn't in my family told me he loved me. I was sixteen years old, and I had only been a believer for a few months. God had providentially connected me with an older friend and mentor named Big Cuz.

One day we were wrapping up a conversation over the phone, and I was caught off guard when he concluded our discussion by saying, "All right, I love you, bro." I *almost* involuntarily said, "I love you too," but instead I followed with an immediate, "All right, bro" and slammed my flip phone shut. I paused, thinking, *What did he just say?*

I felt violated. As far as I was concerned, male friends didn't tell each other they loved them, at least not naturally. If we do express words of affirmation or affection, it's always covert. It's more like (clears throat, deepens voice), "A'ight, man, I uh . . . um . . . Yeah . . . good stuff, bruh." But this was the opposite of that. This grown man on the other end of the phone unashamedly pronounced his brotherly love for me, and man, that moment shaped me! I felt the Holy Spirit prompting me in that moment, asking, *Why is it foreign to say what you feel? Why is it difficult to verbally reveal what you are supposed to experience with your brothers in Christ?*

Paul says to love our brothers "with brotherly affection."[17] In the Christianity of Christ, that is a picture of masculinity. Yet in today's culture, we think in terms of hypermasculinity—some might call it toxic masculinity—that defines the intimacy I've been talking about as a characteristic of the "soft." And one of the consequences of thinking that intimacy is something reserved for erotic relationships with women is that we are experiencing the kind of emptiness and isolation that many of us are living out right now.

WALKING IN THE LIGHT

Few like to be vulnerable, and that is for good reason. Setting aside the way sin and Satan tempt us into isolation, some of our greatest suffering in this life is caused by people who exploit us in our vulnerable space. Vulnerability is a sacred action that requires sacred stewardship. We should not be vulnerable haphazardly. To that end, my community has adopted a practice from my friend Pastor Ray Ortlund that has revolutionized our lives. It's called "walking in the light," and it's based on 1 John 1:6-7: "If we say, 'We have fellowship with him,' and yet we walk in darkness, we are lying and are not practicing the truth. If we walk in the light as he himself is in the light, we have fellowship with one another, and the blood of Jesus his Son cleanses us from all sin."

The passage begins by describing fellowship with God and how that fellowship with Him is compromised when we walk in darkness. But if we walk in the light, then we have fellowship with— you would think the text would say God, but it throws a curveball and says *with one another*. That is fascinating to me! Walking in the light, not running PR for our sin but exposing it, not only brings us into deep fellowship with God; it takes us into deep fellowship with one another! When we become the kind of folks who are willing to confess the sins we are struggling with, the weaknesses we are trying to overcome, and the susceptibility that is plaguing us, we are basically turning our back on friendship with our sin and choosing instead friendship with our God—the sustainer of friendship with each other. In essence, we are proclaiming that we are not on sin's side but rather that we are willing to snitch on it and to talk freely about it with trusted believers around us.

Almost weekly during our small group time, each of us will take a moment and steal away with another member of the group. We then prayerfully and sincerely confess what we are struggling with. No counseling allowed, no book recommendations, only prayer. We invite the Holy Spirit to join us in the light, and we leave transformation to Him. It's always scary, but we can do this because we know that Jesus has forgiven us and His righteousness will cover us. And by God's grace, after many years of "walking in the light," we have had zero instances of anyone's confession leaving the group. Pastor Ray Ortlund has the same testimony. Zero leaks. We've so longed to have a space where we

> YOU ARE ONLY AS CLOSE TO SOMEBODY AS THE EXTENT TO WHICH YOU ARE WILLING TO BE VULNERABLE WITH THEM, EVEN WHEN IT'S MESSY.

can be soul naked that the thought of jeopardizing this sacred space is all but impossible to its participants. This is transparency. This is true intimacy with other believers.

One of the reasons our friendships are often so shallow is because we won't walk in the light that's necessary to deepen them. But you are only as close to somebody as the extent to which you are willing to be vulnerable with them, even when it's messy. If I can parrot Pastor Ray Ortlund one more time, he says, "You can be impressive, or you can be known. But you can't be both."[18] Make it look like you've got it all together or enter into deep relationship with God and others—you can't have both.

It's the messy parts of who we are that we want Jesus to breathe on, but Jesus will never breathe on those parts of our lives if we enter the Christian community closed off to others. We cannot enter the community wrapped in a kind of Christian plastic that keeps ourselves at a "safe" distance or in a hardened cast that keeps things from touching our brokenness. Our brokenness will be protected, but after a while our faith will atrophy. Shallow Christian community results in a surface-level relationship with God, lacking the deep roots necessary for soul nourishment.

Brothers and sisters, sinners need to be allowed to be sinners in our churches. None of us needs to be Jesus in the faith community. Jesus is already doing a good job at that. We just need to trust Him. And one of the best ways to trust in Jesus fully is to confess to others all the ways we are not like Him. Then *He* becomes the impressive one.

I realize what I am saying may feel unrealistic. It is definitely difficult. Vulnerability always is. But without it— without a willingness to stand before each other naked and unashamed, to bear one another's burdens, to embrace

> **ONE OF THE BEST WAYS TO TRUST IN JESUS FULLY IS TO CONFESS TO OTHERS ALL THE WAYS WE ARE NOT LIKE HIM.**

each other's frailties, and to lift one another up—what is the point of being in a community of believers?

I am reminded of this powerful letter a sister wrote to her church years ago:

Dear Church,
    I remember the first time I met you. . . . I simply adored you. . . .
    My, how things have changed.
    I'm now in my 30s, single and in a predominantly white church. I don't fit in anywhere; not with the married couples, the students, the young adults, the older generation or even the children!

She describes trying to form relationships at church, but "everybody wants to talk to those like them." This was especially difficult for her because after converting from Sikhism, she lost her community and her support network. Despite trying home groups and introducing herself to new people, deep friendships seemed out of reach. She concludes by saying, "Maybe a revolution is on the way, a church I dream of; a church for all creeds, for the broken, messed up and hurting. Not a church that merely talks about welcoming everyone, but a church that actually does it."[19]

Her letter is full of hurt and grief, and it breaks my heart. If I could respond to this person, I would say, "First of all, I love you and I see you. Your longings are right, and your loneliness is wrong. Keep beating down the door of heaven until God sends revival."

I'd also want to say, "Much of what you have experienced has to do with the fact that many church communities are based on programs and gatherings and not friendship and fellowship." Meeting once a week is not the koinonia the Bible describes. The church is called to lift burdens, tear down strongholds, heal the soul, and preach the gospel via a life lived together. This is good-dangerous friendship available to us in the Christianity of Christ. But too often we settle for a poor copy of it, replacing intimacy with activity and connectedness with once-a-week check-ins. We are not "together" if we never think of each other past Sunday.

I'd also add that part of the problem is that while churches understand orthodoxy (right teaching) and orthopraxy (right actions), we do not talk enough about ortho*pathos*, right feelings. We know we should draw near to each other, and we may even try to draw near to each other, but when personality, perspective, or pinch points make us feel uncomfortable, we too often just get off the "draw near" train.

The reason I've detailed love as sacrifice and connected it to the backbone of biblical friendship is because we have to be willing to overcome feelings that call us to retreat. I don't need God to help me draw near to people who share all my preferences; I need God to show me that what I share in common with my brothers and sisters in Christ is always more compelling than where we differ.

Forgiveness, reconciliation, and conflict resolution don't happen by switching friends—what the world has taught us is the safer option. And just because someone doesn't immediately add all the "vibes" to our lives (which might say more about us than them) doesn't mean God has no purpose for us in their life. If we lean into the discomfort, associate with the lowly, and make friends with the overlooked, we may see that we experience the presence of God like never before, because that is exactly what He has done in His friendship with us.

I've been told, "You ain't gotta like each other to love each other." Maybe there is some truth in that. But if you love something, you will find ways to like it. Love finds ways to enjoy others, even if there are disagreeable things about the other person. We may not be able to control how we feel, but we are not slaves to our feelings. Often we can influence our hearts with our heads, and if reminding our hearts of Jesus doesn't work, we can also influence our hearts with our hands. In response to aversion or offense, we don't have to follow our hearts; we can *lead* our hearts by doing what is right.

The community of friends can be an intimidating reality, but there's nothing but joy for us on the other side.

The more that we expose our sins, temptations, and shortcomings to the light, the more we will be able to guard ourselves against the things that make sense in seclusion but ultimately lead to our deterioration and keep us from furthering and experiencing the Christianity of Christ. When we are open in friendships to others, when we truly reveal our inner workings and inclinations, we are made more whole and complete. And that, brothers and sisters, makes us the dangerous kind of church that not even the gates of hell can stand against.

CHAPTER 8

DANGEROUS BLESSINGS

I got a God, don't change with the season.
"10K"

The pure Christianity of Christ "hits different."

We cannot follow Jesus for who He is and *not* experience the power of what He does. It is impossible. This Jesus is so dangerously good that to see Him for His beauty, His glory, His brilliance, His kindness, His justice, and His peace is to become obsessed with what you see. I am nothing but a tour guide taking you through all the attractions of the living God. Look, taste, and see—He is good. Let the Christianity of Christ loose, and devils flee. People are rescued and healed. I believe that because I've lived that!

One of the places we see some of this glory is at conferences. I have been to some Christian conferences where the preaching was so on fire and God seemed so near that I literally wanted to sell everything I owned and move to some country in the developing world and preach Jesus all day! The problem is, I only felt that way for about two days. Then I went right back to being the guy I was before the conference. Conferences, for better or for worse, often provide an adrenaline rush of Jesus—the kind of rush that is born in super inspiring moments. But if all we are is a collection of inspirational moments, then we are only ever as good as our last or next rush. Not to hate on conferences, but they can easily turn into fixes. What we need is not an adrenal faith but a cardiovascular faith.

A heart has moments of high intensity, moments of low intensity, and even moments of irregularities, but it keeps on beating to the end. Brothers and sisters, we can indeed live out all the dimensions of the pure Christianity of Christ and experience mountaintops of victory and cultural impact, but that will not erase our valleys of doubt, discouragement, and failure. The question is, When the adrenaline of the mountaintop fades, will we persist in the valley? What about when it simply feels like "this Jesus stuff isn't working"? When things are failing, does that mean God is failing us?

A TALE OF TWO FLIGHTS

At the beginning of 2020, my lovely wife was due to give birth to our third child, baby Nala. I had been doing gymnastics with my schedule for weeks anticipating this baby's arrival, canceling several concerts and upsetting a lot of people. It got to the point where I found myself trying to reason with the baby through my wife's stomach, like, "Come on, Nala. Daddy loves you, but he's got stuff to do."

So after Nala gave us multiple pump fakes, I decided to take my own shot and sneak off to Nashville for a show. *It's just one night*, I thought. *I'll be right back* . . . I thought.

Even though it was only January, it was still 2020, and everyone who lived through 2020 knows that 2020 had a way of being 2020. So naturally, as soon as the plane door closed, I got a text from Michelle. "I think this is it. I'm going into labor."

As the flight attendants made their final preparations, I weighed my options. I was torn between faking a heart attack and storming the cockpit, begging the pilot to stop. Certain that both options would likely end in imprisonment, I decided my best option was to communicate as best I could with my family on the ground and commission Sam, my tour manager, to get me on the first thing smoking back to Tampa.

As soon as we were in the air, I bought the twenty-dollar in-flight Wi-Fi and started texting my wife's sister, Damylett, for labor updates and Sam for flight options. I had him checking other airlines, private flights—anything he could find.

Right about the time Michelle and Damylett left for the hospital, Sam texted me: "I've got a flight for you, but it's going to be really close. You literally have to be the first person off that plane or you're not going to make it." I told him to book it. The next two hours were the longest of my life.

As the pilot began the initial descent, I hit the flight attendant button. When the flight attendant had finally made her way back to me, I said, "Ma'am, my wife is in labor. There's a flight I can catch back home if I'm the first person off this plane. Could you get me to the front when the plane lands?"

She hesitated. "Ah . . . I don't know about that, sir. There's a lot of people in front of you. We'll have to see what we can do." Then she walked back to the front of the plane.

Now, I'm a pretty seasoned traveler. I've logged hundreds of thousands of miles in the air, so I know for a fact that flight attendants can escort passengers to the front of the plane in emergency situations. But somehow I got the impression she didn't believe me. And having been fighting tears the whole flight, I lacked the emotional capacity to defend myself.

By the time the "please return your seats and tray tables to their full upright positions" announcement came over the PA, I felt defeated.

By God's providence, I happened to be sitting next to a group of slightly inebriated middle-aged white women. They had been very vocal the whole flight. They were a lively bunch, like the ladies you see in an airport wearing matching T-shirts on their way to Disney World. I assumed they were on their way home from a bachelorette party. Well, one of them overheard my conversation with the flight attendant and asked me very directly, "What's going on?"

I said, "Yeah, my wife is in labor, and there's a connecting flight I can catch, but I need to get off this plane first, and the flight attendant is not sure if she can help me."

"Wait a minute," she said, almost cutting me off. "You're on a business trip, and you're going to cancel the whole thing and rush home to be with your wife?"

I nodded and she sat back in her seat and shook her head. "That is the sweetest thing I've ever heard. My husband would *never* do that for me."

"Don't you worry about a thing, honey," the woman next to me said. "We are getting you off this flight!" Then she announced to the whole plane, "Everyone, this young man's wife is in labor, so we all need to stay seated and let him get off first!"

I'm telling you, that was it. These ladies were all-in. They were going to get me off that plane if they had to carry me off themselves. And nobody on that flight was pushing back.

The flight attendant, seeing that the women had taken up my cause, suddenly had a change of heart, got back on the intercom, and said, "Everyone, the passenger in 36A's wife is in labor. Can you please hold your seat when we land and let him deplane first?" Then she paused and said, "Matter of fact, let's give him a round of applause."

The entire cabin clapped, and I started crying. Once we stopped, I stood up and the entire cabin clapped again as I made my way to the front of the plane, wiping tears from my eyes.

As soon as I got into the terminal, I called my sister-in-law to let her know I was on my way, but it was too late. Michelle had already started pushing. So rather than taking that flight home, I found a quiet corner, Damylett FaceTimed me, and I phone-coached Michelle through the birth, tearfully shouting encouragement. "C'mon, baby. God is with you! Breathe, push, pull, go!"

Ten minutes later, I saw my beautiful baby girl, Nala, enter the world via the miracle of FaceTime. I told Michelle that she was beautiful and that I loved her and that I would be there as soon as I possibly could. Then I ended the call and sat on the floor for a few more minutes and wept. I was grateful that baby Nala was finally here and that my wife was safe. But I also felt an overwhelming sense of discouragement. I couldn't believe I had missed the birth of my own child. All I could think was, *I was literally just there. If I had waited in the terminal back in Tampa for just fifteen more minutes, I would have gotten Michelle's call in time. Why, God, why?*

When I finally got to the hospital, I was frantically trying to find Michelle's room when a group of nurses stopped me in the hall.

"Are you the husband that called in on FaceTime?" one of them asked.

"Yeah," I said, scanning the walls for room numbers.

"We just want to say thank you," she said.

"We thought it was just awesome," another one chimed in. "Please let us know if there's anything you need."

"Thank you," I said. "I just really wanna see my wife."

"Of course." She smiled and led me to Michelle's room.

It was kind of a strange exchange, but I didn't think much of it until I was settled in with Michelle and holding baby Nala and my sister-in-law gave me some context.

"The nurses were all so moved by the things you said over FaceTime," Damylett said. "One of them actually stepped away after the delivery and broke down."

"Really?" I had been so focused on Michelle during that call, it never occurred to me that other people in the room might be listening in.

"Yeah," Michelle said. "She said she hadn't seen love like that from a husband in a long time."

I looked over at my sister-in-law and said, "Thank you for patching me in and for being here for Michelle. I really appreciate it."

"No," she said, "thank *you*. I'm just so glad I got to be here." I could tell she was really moved. They both were.

That's when I realized God had orchestrated this entire thing. Michelle and Damylett had been needing a moment of connection like this for a long time, and it never would have happened if I had been there. And clearly, the nurses were impacted by whatever I said during that FaceTime call. Not that I wouldn't have been just as supportive had I been present for the birth, but there seemed to be something extra special in the fact that I still found a way to be there for Michelle even though I was six hundred miles away. Even the slightly inebriated woman on the plane was moved by it.

It was obvious that the Lord had something He wanted to either say or show to all of them. My missing that call and scrambling to find a way back home was all part of His plan. And even though I didn't make it back in time, I didn't really lose anything. I still got to be with Michelle during the delivery, and both my wife and our little girl came through the delivery safe and healthy. It was almost as if God was saying to me, "Son, I know how to take care of your wife without you. Trust Me." My story had a happy ending.

A few years earlier, a good and godly friend of mine found himself in a similar situation. Tedashii was, and still is, a well-known rapper and influencer, and he was away from home doing a show when he got a frantic call from his wife telling him that their one-year-old son, Chase, had contracted pneumonia. Tedashii left his concert and jumped on the first flight he could find to be with his wife and son. As soon as he landed, he turned his phone back on and received the worst call a parent could ever imagine. On the other end of the phone was his sobbing wife. The doctor's efforts had been unsuccessful. Chase didn't make it. No immediate silver lining of redemption or discernible purpose—just "my son is gone."

When you think about these two stories side by side, I ask you, who among us is considered blessed? Has the love of God fallen on me but somehow missed my brother in Christ? Does one of us have more of God's favor than the other?

These two stories represent an important juxtaposition, because we seem to only talk about the neat, easily explainable, dot-connecting stories of God working things together for good. But what about the other guy—the one left sitting in absolute darkness and confusion? Is he still loved by God? Is he still blessed, even as he sits in darkness?

These are important questions to reckon with because, brothers and sisters, at some point we will *all* be the other guy.

LOOKING AT 2020 IN 20/20

When the COVID-19 global pandemic hit in 2020, we saw two distinctly different audiences. In one, we saw a group of individuals who were inconvenienced by the pandemic but could see how God was using it to help things go well in their lives. They were like, "Yes, we've been inconvenienced, but at least we're getting to spend more time with our kids, I'm working from home, and we're going to be okay. God is good." Some people even made a small fortune as a result of the pandemic—especially if they had stock in Zoom or owned an e-commerce store. Everyone was forced to conference and shop from home. As the superstar rap trio Migos put it, some of us "turned the pandemic into a bandemic." But there's another story—a story of believers who buried loved ones, who were buried themselves, who lost their jobs, and who are still suffering from the various consequences of the economic, medical, racial, political, and ecclesial disaster that was 2020. Where is the blessed life of the believer living in the second story?

I remember running across Psalm 4:6 at the end of 2020 and being struck by its relevance. It reads, "Many are asking, 'Who can show us anything good?'"[1] Isn't that all of us? Isn't this what we'd been saying all year? Mass unemployment, racial injustice, political chaos, murder hornets—logging on to Twitter was like bracing myself for the next wave of suffering. We are right, dear brothers and sisters, to want the distress to end. In fact, David starts this psalm essentially saying, "God, help me. I am in distress."

Better times are a good desire, but there is something even better than our difficulties ending. David says, "Let the light of your face shine on us, LORD."[2] In other words, give us Your presence. This is the heart of the psalmist! We see it when he says, "But as for me, God's presence is my good,"[3] and "Your faithful love is better than life,"[4] and "It was good for me to be afflicted so that I could learn your statutes."[5]

David says later in Psalm 4, "You have put more joy in my heart than they have when their grain and wine abound."[6] In other words, better times are not the promised land; the presence of God is! When our circumstances have engineered our lives in such a way that we have been brought to the feet of Jesus to know Him not only as the one who heals but also as the one who holds, *then* we are blessed. As Joni Eareckson Tada, who is quadriplegic, says, "Maybe the truly handicapped people are the ones who don't need God as much."[7]

Excuse the Black preacher deep down in my soul, but what if instead of just trying to get out of the 2020s in our lives, we asked what those 2020s are trying to get out of us?

What is God trying to produce in *you*?

VICTORIOUS LIFE

In a lot of ways, many of us are stuck in what I call the gospel of winning. We believe Christianity is about loving God, being faithful, and then Him raining W's down on us. Unfortunately, I am not exempt. And Christian culture often reinforces that idea. This is, in a lot of ways, the conundrum of the Instagram "celebrity preacher," with subtle messages of

The real fruit of righteousness is the presence of God, not necessarily the presence of God's gifts.

- "Look how faithful I've been and what God has done, giving me this massive following."
- "Look at my weekly announcement of some impossible accomplishment we've achieved because of our faith!"
- "Look at my attractive wife, model family, and designer clothes! This is what faith affords!"
- "Look at all these important people that I get to hang with!"

If we are not careful, these aesthetics can be mistaken for the fruit of righteousness. But the fact of the matter is, the real fruit of righteousness is the presence of God, not necessarily the presence of God's gifts, as good as God's gifts are.

The gospel of winning is not sufficient to save us when everything is falling down around us. It looks good for likes, but it will not be good for the long haul. Because the absence of W's is not the absence of God's blessing, it's often a prime occasion for God's presence.

I have never met a brother or sister who has said, "I really loved Jesus before I hit a million followers, but after I hit a million, my faith just shot through the roof." And I don't know a single Christian that is better off spiritually as a result of fame—not one. Popularity is not anointing. And the unreliable blessing of popularity has spoiled into a curse for the many Christian leaders who lost everything after making the presence of popularity more important than the presence of God. Spurgeon was right when he said, "Christians are not so much in danger when they are persecuted as when they are admired."[8]

That's not to say that fame is evil. If you're a rapper like me, you don't have a job without fame. In similar fashion, there is tremendous blessing in enjoying your life! But do not attach the potency of the favor, blessing, and presence of God to things that will pass away. Likewise, do not think that God is *not* blessing you because you lack the trimmings and trappings of an Instagram pastor. Remember, the absence of W's is not the absence of the presence of God.

I watched Tedashii endure a long battle with sorrow after burying his son. And when he said to me, "God is still good," it had weight to it. It sounded like a man who found out God was good by meeting Him, not by repeating a slogan. Burying a child is perhaps Satan's chief expression of this evil age. But when Tedashii says that God is good, he is saying, "He is still God in my life. He has not left us. He is still loving me. This is not the end. I will hold my baby again." Our God, in a profound way, is "near to the brokenhearted."[9]

When I was a child, my mother taught me a prayer. I said it every night for years:

Now I lay me down to sleep. I pray the Lord my soul to keep.
If I die before I wake, I pray the Lord my soul to take.

As I got older, I stopped saying that prayer because it seemed weird to have children anticipate their death before they went to bed. Generally, death is not something normal people want to think about. We understandably want to distance ourselves from death. We see death as something that happens to *other people*, not *me*. Yet Moses prays, "Teach us to number our days that we may get a heart of wisdom."[10] There is something about being brought near to death that strikes wisdom in a man or woman. Tragedy makes us face our own mortality. And there can be grace in that.

As Matthew McCullough, who wrote the incredibly helpful book *Remember Death*, said, "So long as death remains someone else's problem, Jesus will remain someone else's Savior."[11] The gospel doesn't turn off in times of distress; it turns up.

There are going to be moments when our bodies break, when our situations break, when our hearts break. Things are not always going to be put together. But just because everything is not put together or things are falling apart doesn't mean that God has forgotten us. Believing that success equates to blessings and tragedy is the lack of God's presence or favor in your life is the Christianity of the Land. That is dangerous thinking! And it is wrong thinking.

I have heard people say that the one prayer we can be assured will always be answered is "Thy will be done." We just don't always like the will of God. We won't always be comfortable with it. But no matter the outcome, God's will *will* always result in your blessing.

I don't want to romanticize tragedy, but dear brothers and sisters, your tragedy is not a spiritual disadvantage. Our God is so fly that He can use our tragedies as spiritual accelerants. We just cannot give up.

WHAT DOES IT MEAN TO BE BLESSED?

When Jesus delivered His Sermon on the Mount, He gave us the Beatitudes, His supreme blessings. If we were to rewrite them based on how we live today, we would probably say, "Blessed are the rich, blessed are the comfortable, blessed are the strong, blessed are the well followed."

But Jesus said, "Blessed are the poor. Blessed are the brokenhearted. Blessed are the meek. Blessed are those who are hungry and thirsty for righteousness. Blessed are the persecuted."[12] Why? Because that's where God is. He is the God of the weak and the vulnerable and the hurting. If that's what we've become, it is a blessing because it's an opportunity for us to come closer to God.

Poverty in itself is not a blessing. What Jesus is saying is that God can still bless you *beyond* your poverty, by teaching you, forming you, strengthening you through your situation and bringing you to a place where you not only have a closer relationship with God, but you also have more grace, mercy, compassion, and understanding for others who are suffering.

We will have peaks and we will have valleys, and God is present in both. We all, to some extent, crave predictability and consistency. We want to be able to live stable lives, but it's difficult to capture that when everything around us is constantly changing. God, however, never changes, and to be filled with His presence is to have an unshakable existence.

Paul says, "I know how to make do with little, and I know how to make do with a lot. In any and all circumstances I have learned the secret of being content—whether well fed or hungry, whether in abundance or in need. I am able to do all things through him who strengthens me."[13]

Likewise, in Proverbs, Agur says, "Give me neither poverty nor wealth, feed me with the food I need. Otherwise, I might have too much and deny you, saying, 'Who is the LORD?'"[14]

Brothers and sisters, the blessed life is being able to find the spirit of peace in a world of uncertainty. If I could put that sentiment in a bottle and sell it, I'd be a trillionaire. Most businesses exist because they offer some semblance of that very idea. God offers us this blessed life in Him. This is the good-dangerous Christianity of Christ. Even when our circumstances are what the world would call cursed, we can remain unswerving and unshakable with our eyes firmly fixed on God because He meets us where we are and is responsible for our destiny. And that destiny is blessing. The Christianity of Christ keeps us standing even when we are not covered in the temporary W's we all desperately want because some of His most important work happens when those W's are not raining down on us.

> **THE BLESSED LIFE IS BEING ABLE TO FIND THE SPIRIT OF PEACE IN A WORLD OF UNCERTAINTY.**

THE FINAL W

Jesus said, "In the world you will have tribulation." There will be poverty. There will be sickness. There will be racial injustice. Some of us will bury our children, our parents, our spouses, our friends. But that does not mean we are not loved, that God is not smiling upon us. Because Jesus also says, "Take heart; I have overcome the world."[15]

I opened this chapter with a story about two journeys, one ending in life and one ending in loss. I am going to close with a story about another journey that ended with both.

It is the story of Lazarus told in John 11. The mood of the passage is heavy. There is a lot of weeping and mourning. Heartbreak is near. Jesus is going to be crucified in a few days. The people He has come to save want Him dead. And to top that off, His dear friend—a man named Lazarus—is sick.

Fearing the end is near, Lazarus's sisters, Mary and Martha, send a message to Jesus: "Lord, the one you love is sick."[16] But Jesus doesn't come. In fact, He stays away for two more days. When Jesus finally does arrive in Lazarus's hometown of Bethany, He finds that Lazarus has already been in the tomb for four days.

Martha and Mary are in absolute agony. They have watched their brother die, and in the back of their minds, they have to be wondering, *Why didn't Jesus show up to help Lazarus? Most of the time Jesus is out healing strangers. Why would He turn His back on His friend?*

When Jesus shows up, Martha confronts Him immediately, exclaiming, "Lord, if you had been here, my brother wouldn't have died."[17] Moments later, Mary rushes out to see Jesus, falls at His feet, and echoes her sister's complaint.

It reminds me of the time I watched an atheist sitting on stage with one of my favorite pastors talking about why he doesn't believe anymore. He cited the Holocaust, which saw six million Jews put to death along with seventy-four million others by the time the war was over. Then he turned to the pastor and said, "Where was God?" It's the same question Mary and Martha ask. And it's a fair question. *Where were You?*

One of the great failings of the Christianity of the Land is how quiet it can be in the face of suffering. I don't want a gospel that has plenty to say in times of abundance but is mute in times of famine. A gospel that has plenty to say when we're on the mountaintop but nothing to say when we're in the valley. That God is visible only when we're celebrating and ghosts us when we're suffering.

God is not indifferent to our suffering any more than Jesus is indifferent to the news of Lazarus's illness. In fact, God takes our pain and suffering so seriously that He was willing to take it on Himself. He doesn't just observe our pain. He wrapped Himself in it. God cares about our suffering so much that He became a man and suffered it Himself. Where is God in our suffering? He is suffering right along with us!

GOD TAKES OUR PAIN AND SUFFERING SO SERIOUSLY THAT HE WAS WILLING TO TAKE IT ON HIMSELF.

Back to our friend Lazarus. What Mary and Martha do not know is that when Jesus received their message, His response was not indifference or ambivalence. Indeed, it was the opposite. When He heard that His dear friend was sick, He said, "This sickness will not end in death but is for the glory of God, so that the Son of God may be glorified through it."[18]

There is a lesson in that. Just because Jesus doesn't show up when we want Him to does not mean He doesn't love us. It just means He has something better in mind—namely, the glory of God.

Brothers and sisters, you know how this story ends. Lazarus's sickness does not end in death. It does not end in victory for Satan. Jesus goes to Lazarus's tomb and literally calls His friend out of the grave. And the moment Lazarus walks out of that tomb, his death becomes a victory for Christ. Let me say that again: Lazarus's death ultimately was not a victory for Satan. It was not a result of the absence of God. It was for the glory of God.

Folks that follow me know the name of my universe—HGA (His Glory Alone). It is said that if God had a nickname, it would be Glory, because that is the most common word used to praise God in the Bible. It is the most accurate word to describe what is happening when you are in the presence of the living God. And it is the most accurate way to describe Lazarus walking out of that tomb after being stone-cold dead for four days—glorious! All that Lazarus had suffered in sickness and lost in death took a back seat to the fact that Lazarus was now alive!

Before He called Lazarus out of the tomb, Jesus said to Martha, "Didn't I tell you that if you believed you would see the glory of God?"[19] That is His promise to all of us—His blessing on all of us. If we believe, we will have eternal life. We will see and experience the glory of God. This story of eternal life is bigger than Lazarus. And it has to be. Because as impressive as it was for Lazarus to be raised from the dead, he most certainly died again. Jesus told Martha, "I am the resurrection and the life. The one who believes in me, even if he dies, will live."[20] Note Jesus doesn't say He knows how to resurrect but that He *is* the resurrection. The true power of the story of Lazarus is not Lazarus; he points to what it means to belong to Jesus. Jesus is the resurrection, and those that die trusting Him will experience a resurrection to life and can never die again—because Jesus will never die again. What Lazarus experienced in part we will have in whole forever.

Pain will not win.

Suffering will not win.

Death will not win.

The resurrection will have the final word.

THE WEIGHT OF GLORY

I have three babies. My wife delivered all of them naturally, and after watching her suffer the pain of labor, I had always wondered why. One day I asked her, and she said, "The pain is only temporary. Then I get a baby, and there's something about the pain you experience that helps you to appreciate what you are holding in your hands."

My wife is right. Pain is temporary. Brothers and sisters, our dual challenge when suffering comes our way is not only to figure a way out of it but to sit in the distress and ask God, *What are You trying to get out of me? What might You be trying to produce in me? How are You meeting me here? Because I know You are in the room.*

Think about the audacity of Paul: "For this light momentary affliction is preparing for us an eternal weight of glory beyond all comparison."[21] Do you realize how offensive that statement is if it is not true? How insensitive can Paul be? How could you call nearly a million people dead of COVID-19 in America alone (at the time of writing) or the burial of a child "light" and "momentary"?

The only way this makes sense is if Paul knows a kind of glory that is so big, so healing, and so redemptive that it will make our greatest losses seem small. What worked against us will work for us. God is preparing an eternal weight of beauty that is heavier than all the combined ugly in this world. Paul speaks like this because he knows that those losses are not just lessons; they are leverage for eternal gain.

The glory that awaits us in the place we will be the longest— eternity with our God—will be so profound, so all-inclusive, so wonderful that it will not only give us joy forever moving forward, it will turn around and make right all we have lost in this life.

We will not stand before God thanking Him that we had as little trouble in this life as possible. We will kiss the difficulties that we rightfully hated because they did nothing but maximize our eternal reward in the presence of our King!

To buy into the Christianity of the Land is to buy into a false, superficial view of victory and achievement, loss and suffering. The dangerous Christianity of Christ is the blessed hope of humanity amid our deepest struggles. Never let it go!

CHAPTER 9

DANGEROUS JOY

My wife happy and Jesus love me ain't nothing left to conform to.
"NO CHAINS"

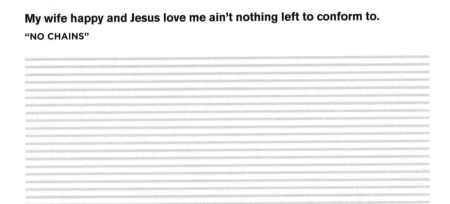

Before I met Jesus, you couldn't convince me that God wasn't boring and that Jesus didn't drain all the fun out of life. Every time I walked into the sanctuary of a church, it felt like the spirit of NyQuil would attack me. It was almost as if the preaching helped me sleep better. Even the "cool Christian stuff" for young people was annoying. It was all like, "Look! We are fun! We have pizza parties, PG movies, and Christian versions of everything in the world! Try this can of 'Spirit'! It tastes just like Sprite!" Yeah . . . miss me with that.

But when the Lord opened my eyes to His glory, power, and goodness, I quickly realized that the competitive edge for Christianity was not the "cool stuff"; it was God. It always has been. I just didn't see it. It's like a blind man complaining that he's bored in the Sistine Chapel. There's nothing wrong with the art. He just can't see it. If he could, he wouldn't be able to look away.

I recall something that happened in Chicago a few years ago. I love deep-dish pizza, so whenever we're in the Windy City, we go to Lou Malnati's. That's not product placement; I just really love that place. I was excited to get a few deep-dish pizzas for the whole band, and they loved every bite—with the exception of my road manager. Upon tasting this gift from God baked to holy perfection, the gentleman said, "This is pretty good, but it's no Little Caesars."

I kid you not. I was on the phone with my wife at the time, and as soon as he said it, I was like, "Babe, I got to call you back." I hung up the phone and said, "What did you just say?" He looked at the pizza, then looked up at me, and said, "It's good, but it's no Little Caesars." After deciding that firing him on the spot would be inappropriate, I said to him, "Listen, brother. The problem is not the pizza. The problem is your taste buds."

There has never been a lack or deficiency in the flavor of experiencing God. We just lack the taste buds to savor His goodness.

I remember the time I met NBA superstar Steph Curry. I was doing a concert in the Bay Area with my friend Trip Lee, and Steph came to the show. Not only did I not know who he was, he was dressed almost exactly like the security guards working the venue. So when I saw him standing there all alone, I walked right up, patted him on the shoulder, and said, "God bless, and thanks for helping us out." Then I went about my day. Now, I try to treat everyone the same, but giving honor where honor is due requires recognizing who you are dealing with. And if you are ignorant about who someone is, you won't honor them the way you should.

TO BE UNIMPRESSED WITH GOD IS TO BE IGNORANT OF WHO HE IS.

So it is with God. To be unimpressed with God is to be ignorant of who He is. Full stop. God is the originator and sustainer of all things true, good, and beautiful. If something is good, it is borrowed from God. From marriage to mangoes, fatherhood to fashion, faith to fitness—though the level of importance may vary, all these things are bread crumbs rolling off the very table of the living God.

Randy Alcorn, in his book *Heaven*, writes, "Our desire for pleasure and the experience of joy come directly from God's hand. He made our taste buds, adrenaline, sex drives, and the nerve endings that convey pleasure to our brains. Likewise, our imaginations and our capacity for joy and exhilaration were made by the very God we accuse of being boring."[1]

This is why it bothers me so much that Christianity is often known as the religion of killjoy, as if God filled the world with all kinds of pleasures for everyone *except* His people to enjoy. If I can tip my hand a little, that is nonsense—emphatically not the Christianity of Christ. What we find in the living God is not the end of happiness but the source of happiness. Likewise, the Christianity of Christ does not prohibit us from enjoying our lives; it is indeed the *best* way to enjoy our lives.

If we don't see God in a good steak, if we don't see God in an enjoyable evening with our family and friends, if we don't see God in the smile of someone we love, if we don't see God in moments of beauty, then we don't understand God.

ALL OR NOTHING?

Not long after I accepted Christ, I broke up with my high school sweetheart, stopped hanging out with a lot of my old friends—I even stopped listening to mainstream hip-hop. I didn't want to listen to anything that wasn't nourishing my soul. If it didn't bring me closer to God, it was not welcome on my playlist. There was a lot of value in that, especially early in my walk, but I started slipping to extremes. I started studying the history of the persecuted church and felt as though I needed a harder life to be more authentic. I swung hardcore into what is known as poverty theology, where I found virtue in being nothing and having nothing. I read the excellent *Foxe's Book of Martyrs*, subscribed to the powerful *Voice of the Martyrs* magazine, and committed myself to joining the fellowship of suffering—even if I had to engineer that suffering. I literally fasted twice a week for months, which is not necessarily bad, but I kept a box of cookies close by to make it harder for myself.

I think a lot of people have that experience when they first become Christians. For the rich young ruler to follow Jesus, it meant giving up his many possessions. There is value in considering how I might part with things that defined me before to prove that these things don't have power over me, because I have a new Lord now. I'll do anything for Him. While I did go through that, I did it joyfully, and God would often meet me in my overzealousness. I would read the Bible for four, sometimes five hours a day. I cherish those times. But as I matured in my faith, I came to realize that I could enjoy God not only in His Word but in His world as well.

One of the greatest threats to the Christianity of Christ is the misguided belief that following Jesus means giving up every conceivable earthly pleasure in the name of piety. The problem with that is too often people believe that not only should we be resisting evil, we should equally be resisting good. Though there is great power in controlling our appetites, giving up the good things we enjoy does not always equal nearness to God. I've spent a lot of time in this book talking about decentering self, but I do not want to overlook God's call to be instructed on how to love your neighbor by considering the way you love yourself.[2] Self-love is good as long as it doesn't stop at self or permit the evil that self might desire. If in the name of loving God we refuse to love ourselves by enjoying good things, we are literally cutting ourselves off from a whole world of experiences that were meant to nourish our faith and increase our love for God.

The problem with the Christianity of the Land is that it cares more about presentation than it does about transformation. You've got folks that don't drink, don't curse, and don't club, but they also don't love. Self-denial has an important place in the Christianity of Christ, but never forget that the Garden of Eden had a single tree that was off limits—just one, among what would have been thousands. I'm convinced there is always more to enjoy than there is to deny.

That said, are there certain songs we shouldn't listen to and certain movies we shouldn't watch? Certainly. But when you're in a transformative relationship with God, not listening to certain songs or watching certain shows is not about killing your joy; it's about protecting it. Furthermore, our enjoyment of the arts will vary from believer to believer, depending on how our conscience alerts us in the moment. There is wisdom in not first asking "Is this Christian?" but rather, "Is it good and does this threaten my joy in Jesus?"

So while there *is* merit in not drowning ourselves in the pursuit of decadence, we don't have to live under a bridge and beat ourselves with a stick every day. As A. W. Tozer said, "The people of God ought to be the happiest people in all the wide world! People should be coming to us constantly and asking the source of our joy and delight."[3]

Take Solomon, for example.

EVERYTHING IS MEANINGLESS?

The book of Ecclesiastes has a reputation as kind of a downer. Solomon starts with the following assessment of the world: "Everything is meaningless, completely meaningless!"[4] Yeah . . . that's pretty bleak. He then goes on to compare the pleasures of creation to the act of grabbing a handful of water and watching as it seeps through your fingers. The longer you hold it, the less you have. The pursuit of success, accomplishments, and wealth are all—according to Solomon—as futile as chasing the wind.

It is easy to take Solomon's words as a condemnation of the pleasures of life. Money, food, drink, entertainment, and the committed pursuit of enjoying life—he assumes all are a waste of time at best. Likewise, many preachers spend the majority of their time spinning caution tape around these areas, telling folks to stay away. On some level, this motivation is justifiable, especially considering how often many of these things are abused. Sadly, part of our fallen condition is our recalcitrance toward moderation. And then there is sin. Human nature often compels us to want the very things we should, for our own good, avoid.

A closer look at the Hebrew text, however, points to a far less fatalistic take on the subject. The Hebrew word translated "meaningless" or "futile" or "vanity" is *hebel*, which literally means "smoke" or "vapor," that which dissipates easily. It is like breath—here for a moment, then quickly gone.

James, for example, tells us that our lives are a "vapor that appears for a little while, then vanishes,"[5] and David proclaims that "a human is like a breath; his days are like a passing shadow."[6] But that is not a pronouncement of the meaninglessness of human life. This is Scripture speaking to the limits of things. It is not, however, speaking to their usefulness. If a hammer is the only thing you have to build a house, your efforts will be futile because you need much more than that. But you will be hard-pressed to get the job done with no hammer at all. The Bible places everything against a backdrop of eternity, making all of life and its contents momentary and transient, but that does not at all suggest that life and its contents are devoid of purpose, meaning, and grace.

If we run with a careless reading of Solomon's proclamation, we create the kind of Christians who define spiritual engagement with God as denying the natural world, where God's presence stops at the door of the earthly. Anything not strictly devotional becomes either tolerated or hated, making God the enemy of "living a little," because he would rather have us fasting and praying. This, by the way, is precisely the reason Christians have authored thousands of books on the spiritual disciplines of prayer and fasting, Bible reading, and

What we find in the living God is not the end of happiness but the source of happiness.

church fellowship (which are immensely important) but far fewer on the discipline of enjoying the life God gave you.

We don't need more caution tape or to simply surrender all that is good. What we need are fences—boundaries that protect us from abusing what is good. Better yet, we need to break the cycle of destructive behavior, not discard entirely the object that is being abused—*especially* when that object is a gift from God.

Solomon's point is not that enjoying life is a waste of time. What is a waste of time is the pursuit of enjoying life without the fear of God. This is why in Proverbs Solomon calls the fear of God "the beginning of wisdom."[7] And by fear, he doesn't mean we are to be terrified of God. He's referring to the serious acknowledgment and perpetual reverence of God's reign over life that keeps us from getting into trouble. For example, I know I can eat one steak, but I also know that if I try to eat three or four of them in one sitting, I'm going to be sick. That doesn't mean I should avoid partaking in a good steak. It just means I have a healthy "fear" of what can happen if I abuse something that is otherwise good. In a similar way the fear of God gives us boundaries which serve as guides to help us enjoy ourselves without destroying ourselves. Ultimately all of those enjoyments are designed to teach us something about the truth, beauty, and goodness of God. This is part of why there is nothing more dangerous than going through life disregarding God. But when God is central, when He is fixed in our hearts, the joys of life are truly ours.

Look at what happens if you keep reading the words of Solomon. He says, "I commended enjoyment because there is nothing better for a person under the sun than to eat, drink, and enjoy himself."[8] Even he acknowledges that the good pleasures of this world should be commended. They are like seasoning. Too much can ruin the dish, but the right amount makes it sing! Solomon is simply saying, make sure God is the chef.

WHAT IN THE WORLD?

In the final days of Jesus' life, John the apostle lets us eavesdrop on what Jesus prays about before His death. He prays about being glorified through His disciples, and He says, "I am not praying that you take them out of the world but that you protect them from the evil one."[9] This is where the popular Christian maxim "In the world, not of the world" comes from. But sometimes Christians focus so much on not being "of the world" that we forget we are designed to be "in the world."

Brothers and sisters, the world, though broken, is still good. Unfortunately, we often see the world like the TV series *The Walking Dead*. We go into the world to get supplies and rescue those in danger, and then we try not to get touched before returning to our bunkers. Not only does Jesus call us to engage the world in proclaiming the gospel, but there is much in the world that we can use for our own spiritual health. In John Piper's book *When I Don't Desire God*, there is a powerful chapter on wielding the world in our fight for joy. In his comments on C. S. Lewis's understanding of the connection between the physical and the spiritual, Piper says,

> Lewis . . . reminds us that spiritual emotions, like joy in God, are only experienced in connection with physical sensations. They are not identical, but they are almost always inseparable. In this earthly life we are never disembodied souls with only spiritual emotions. We are complex spiritual-physical beings who experience joy in Christ as something more, but almost never less, than physical sensation.[10]

The spiritual does not cancel the natural; it leads it. In fact, the spiritual actually pulls the natural into worship, gratitude, and praise. David tells us,

The heavens declare the glory of God,
  and the sky above proclaims his handiwork.
Day to day pours out speech,
  and night to night reveals knowledge.
There is no speech, nor are there words,
  whose voice is not heard.
Their voice goes out through all the earth,
  and their words to the end of the world.[11]

There is real joy in physically looking at the sun, moon, stars, mountains, and oceans and seeing the glory of God's brilliance and beauty on display. The psalmist says, "You have made me rejoice, LORD, by what you have done; I will shout for joy because of the works of your hands."[12]

God's work is all over the place! From the elements in nature to the technology I'm using to write this sentence, we all rejoice in Him, for these things ring of His glory.

Paul tells Timothy that it is "the teachings of demons" to "forbid marriage and demand abstinence from foods that God created to be received with gratitude by those who believe and know the truth. For everything created by God is good, and nothing is to be rejected if it is received with thanksgiving, since it is sanctified by the word of God and by prayer."[13] Isn't it fascinating that Paul calls terminating the good enjoyments of this world demonic? It is indeed our good earthly enjoyments that serve our cause of giving thanks to our God.

We, the people of God, bring tremendous meaning to all good things—*if* we receive them with joyful gratitude, conscious of the presence of God. Prayerfully inviting the work of God into the gifts of life gives things what Piper calls "God-exalting function."[14]

Calvin called it the "Theatrum Dei Gloria," or the "theater of the glory of God."[15] He says, "The whole world is a theater for the display of the divine goodness, wisdom, justice and power."[16] The world is the Lord's. It is subject to evil, but it is not itself evil.

Christianity is not a call to turn off our humanity. In fact, we need a more human Christianity. God didn't make humans to forget they were human. Even in our effort to escape the world and focus on spirituality, we still sing with our vocal cords, pray with our breath, and memorize and meditate on Scripture through neurological processing, all of which are human. To say it more bluntly, you were not made for heaven; you were made for earth. Heaven now is an intermediary place before the second coming of Jesus, but in the end our ultimate home is a new earth, where we will live as glorified humans.

Being human is good because not only did God make humans, but Jesus *became* a human and is still a human to this day. That's part of why we can't find His bones. He was resurrected in a body, and all of His humanity is His forever. As such, His very being underscores the goodness of creation. The spiritual realm and the physical realm are duly upheld in Christ. Jesus became the light that helps us navigate them both. The world is a place beaming with wonder, and we have every God-given right to take part in its awe.

Frank Boreham, a pastor who attended Charles Spurgeon's school, once stated that "the world is not dark, but delightful. Yet it is only delightful because of the lantern."[17] Jesus is the one that illuminates the goodness and wonder of the created world.

Too many Christians are missing the emotional complexities that were very much present in the humanity of Christ because they feel like if they humanize Jesus, they lose Jesus' power. But Jesus' power for us *is* His humanity. The fact that He became one of us means that His saving power touches every bit of our humanity. Every part of me—from my humor and my nerve endings to my passions and desires—are expressions of my ontology, my soul, and my physical body. Jesus lived in all of that. He wrapped Himself in all of that to show that He's going to redeem all of it. Every bit of me will be redeemed—not simply my soul.

Scripture is replete with examples of the intersection of the body and the soul. The story of Elijah and Jezebel is a perfect one. After a glorious victory over the prophets of Baal at Mount Carmel, mocking their gods and calling down fire, the warrior prophet Elijah comes down the mountain flexing the presence of God—until he learns that Jezebel seeks to take his life. Elijah gets so overwhelmed by fear that he flees to the wilderness and falls into a suicidal state, requesting that God end his life. Nervous and uncertain of his future, he falls asleep, likely from physical exhaustion. He is eventually woken by an angel. Instead of the normal "do not be afraid" introduction, the angel simply tells him to eat. Eat, Elijah! That was God's advice. Have you ever felt the spiritual power of taking a nap and getting something to eat?[18]

In his work *The Spirit of the Disciplines*, Dallas Willard points out that "the spiritual and the bodily are by no means opposed in human life—they are complementary."[19] As Christians who affirm the created world and see ourselves as players in the drama of creation, we ought to be good stewards who care for our souls and our bodies. Sometimes eating a snack and taking a nap can be an act of spiritual liberation. Stress and worry are not always the result of a lack of faith but can be a lack of rest and nutrition.

Willard further points out that Scripture is a proponent of wisdom not only for spiritual revitalization but also for physical and psychological healing. According to Willard, "[Paul] clearly perceived and explained the fundamental structures and processes of the human self related to its well-being, its corruption, and its redemption." He goes on to say, "Only the fatal separation of salvation from life in modern thinking makes it possible to separate theology from psychology."[20]

It is clear that Jesus cares for our spiritual, psychological, and physical needs. Even in Scripture we see Jesus healing people's physical disabilities often before He ever approaches their spiritual predicaments. It is not antispiritual to approach physical and psychological problems with prayerful pursuit of physical and psychological solutions. The problem may not be that you don't believe the gospel like you should. You might simply need a therapist.

A few years ago, I was at a church to do a concert, and I needed to reduce the swelling on my vocal cords before the show. I asked our host if they had any ibuprofen. The host looked at me and said, "Why don't you ask God to heal you?" to which I responded, "You don't think God is healing me through the ibuprofen?" We kind of laughed off the situation, but I could not help but think about how, for centuries, saints likely prayed and labored for a remedy for inflammation in the body. It was the church that led the medical field in the Middle Ages. Here we stand centuries later, holding a literal answered prayer in our hands, not assigning the glory to God but to Motrin.

Again, brothers and sisters, we were not made for heaven but for earth—earth redeemed. God provided us with everything necessary to enjoy the splendor of His creation. He purposely gave us sight to observe the beauty in a sunset or a work of art. God intentionally gave us ears to listen to sweet melodies and resounding symphonies. He decisively gave us taste buds to enjoy culinary creations that cause our hearts to rejoice. (You probably can tell by now I'm a foodie.) I love that one of the first things we see Jesus do after His resurrection is eat fish. What tremendous affirmation of the goodness of creation—specifically, a good meal—when Jesus engages in it in His glorified state!

Not only did God provide us with senses, He also formed us with interests. God purposefully gave us minds that love the strategy and science of sports. God formed us with hands so that we might sculpt, embroider, or bring other forms of artistic expression into existence. This is God's doing, God's design, and God's idea. The thrill, pleasure, excitement, and fun that we gain from such activities is not the property of Satan. God fashioned us as humans to interact with the created world so that we might see His

GOD FASHIONED US AS HUMANS TO INTERACT WITH THE CREATED WORLD SO THAT WE MIGHT SEE HIS GLORY IN ALL THAT WE DO.

glory in all that we do. And in all our doing, we bring Him praise. He created this world, He created our human faculties, and He concluded that it is not merely good, but very good!

WHAT'S AT STAKE?

The inability to enjoy life can muster a gray existence for the believer and perhaps allow a foothold for the enemy. In *The Screwtape Letters*, C. S. Lewis describes the importance of practicing things we really enjoy, and he comments on the enemy's goal to distract us from those pleasant delights. A collection of fictional letters written by a head demon, Screwtape, to his apprentice, Wormwood, *The Screwtape Letters* details the progress or setbacks of their "patient," a Christian man they are trying to tempt away from God. In one of the letters addressing Wormwood's failures with the patient, Screwtape says, "You first of all allowed the patient to read a book he really enjoyed. . . . In the second place, you allowed him to walk down to the old mill and have tea there—a walk through the country he really likes." As Screwtape points out, "You allowed him two real positive Pleasures." These pleasures provided the patient with a "touchstone of reality." Screwtape goes on to write that "the man who truly and disinterestedly enjoys any one thing in the world, for its own sake, and without caring two-pence what other people say about it, is by that very fact fore-armed against some of our subtlest modes of attack."[21]

Lewis's description of the man's enjoyment is telling. Christians who drift through life with no zeal, little passion, and an inability to relish the blessings of life are setting themselves up for a strained relationship with joy. This sort of lifestyle is dangerous, as it allows room for the enemy. If the devil wants anything, it is to rob us of taking any pleasure in what God declares good and has placed here for our benefit. This is a tactical approach, because when the fervor of our devotional efforts runs dry, and no other buffer of godly enjoyment is set in place, it is easy for us to turn to sin for comfort or relief. By way of example, Lewis, writing as Screwtape about sexual temptation, states that "the attack has a much better chance of success when the man's whole inner world is drab and cold and empty."[22]

One of the first things a therapist will try to establish for a recovering addict is replacing unhealthy patterns with good alternatives. It's more than simply not committing the sin; it's also replacing the behavior with righteous engagements. I believe this is a sub-principle from Paul's admonishment to take off the old habits of life and "put on the Lord Jesus Christ."[23] Putting on Christ involves prayerful, grateful, Scripture-led engagement with the good things God has created.

We may have been taught to think that doing something for our own enjoyment is selfish, something we need to apologize for or keep to a minimum. But Paul lists joy among the fruit of the Spirit—the markers of the Christian life—second only to love, and we are told in Scripture that "the joy of the LORD is [our] strength."[24] It is in joy that the Christianity of Christ allows us to face the darkness, to become a threat to the threat. Joy truly is our strength. As C. S. Lewis said, "Joy is the serious business of Heaven."[25] As followers of Jesus, it's who we are, what we do, and what we're destined for. When we understand worldly things as gifts from God and tools for furthering the Kingdom, we become better stewards of those very gifts.

GUILT-FREE ENJOYMENT

A lot of Christians will say, "How can I eat at a nice restaurant while there are people starving in the world?" Or "How can I redecorate my house when there are people in the world who are homeless?" To that I say, we are right to think about the fact that there are people starving while we're eating at nice restaurants. But to the Christian who responds to that conundrum by saying, "I just won't eat at five star restaurants," I say, "That's all well and good, but not treating yourself isn't solving world hunger either, is it?"

I don't eat at nice restaurants very often, but when I do, I eat that meal to the glory of God! After all, He created it, and He bestowed someone with the culinary gifts to make it the savory delight that it is. Is it possible that God created that meal for my enjoyment? And isn't the ultimate goal for us to love our God and enjoy Him forever? However, there is no shame in refusing five-star restaurants if it frees me to use my resources to help those that have nothing—especially those I consider neighbors in my church and in my community. But remember that even *that* is a pursuit of joy. There is joy in practicing financial restraint in order to create a capacity to serve that you wouldn't have if you visited an expensive restaurant. It's not a case of either/or; it's both/and. As long as it doesn't obliterate your ability to serve, steward, and sacrifice for others, it is indeed possible to enjoy a fancy meal without guilt. Or, for the sake of meeting a need you wouldn't have capacity for if you were to "live a little," it is good to enjoy the act of sacrificing for others. Amen to both perspectives.

The Bible makes it very clear that our responsibility is not simply to help widows and orphans—even though James says that is true religion.[26] There are a lot of people out there helping widows and orphans that want nothing to do with Jesus. God's heart for us is that, in our love for widows and orphans, our service would be an act of joy, flowing out of a thriving love for our God, knowing Him, and being conformed to His likeness. That is the promised land for us. Seeing the broken restored and the vulnerable advocated for, without overlooking that we are often the broken and the vulnerable in need of help—all of that true religion is designed to be an occasion for more joy. This is a mission for me. I try to remember the words of 1 John 1:4. In all that I pen, I am "writing these things so that our joy may be complete." The chief end of humanity is to be in relationship with the God who made us and to be aligned with the purposes for which we were created.

Given that, I would say that if you have the means to beautify your home, I hope that you will be doing it so that it feels more like a home to your family and that you might be a better host to others and bring others together in Christian fellowship. After all, God decorates the earth all the time in ways that don't feed people. God sees the beauty and enjoys species of animals yet to be discovered and flowers on mountains no human will ever see. He sees it and enjoys it. Decorating our homes is more than beauty for beauty's sake. It is an opportunity to use our resources both for joy and to show God's love to others.

What about money?

Jesus said, "You cannot serve both God and money."[27] Unfortunately, we often take that to mean that money and wealth are inherently wicked. Yes, money is a terrible master, but it can also be a masterful servant. That is why Scripture doesn't demand that we renounce our resources. Rather, it implores us to use them for the glory of God.

There is an old Wesleyan saying that generally goes, "Make as much money as you can, save as much money as you can, and give as much money as you can." In other words, we should work hard so we can provide for our families but also so that we might be generous to others. Like I said earlier, part of being a Christian means I will never have as much money as I would if I wasn't one.

One of the ways we, as Christians, enjoy our money is by giving it away because confronting poverty, funding Kingdom efforts, and ensuring the security of our families is far more enjoyable than just sitting back and watching our bank accounts grow. First John 3:17 declares that "if anyone has this world's goods and sees a fellow believer in need but withholds compassion from him—how does God's love reside in him?"

Having great resources is only a threat to our faith when we fail to realize our resources are His. But if submitted to the agenda of the Kingdom, our resources can become ammunition for the gospel.

The key is striking the right balance and not clinging to money like a savior (which it is most definitely not) or doing what is also harmful, casting it out like a demon.

THE BEST IS YET TO COME

Through recasting Christianity and its relationship with the world around us, we can find substantial, biblical joy in this life in ways that bring glory to Christ. But in it all, our eyes must stay fixed on the coming redemption of things and the coming destiny of when the new heaven and the new earth replace the old. Why? Because joy in this life will be perpetually illusive, fragmented, and incomplete. Hope in eternity matters because we will never achieve the life we've always hoped for. There will be injustices that will go unremedied, wounds only heaven will heal, impediments and tragedies that disrupt our enjoyments. Joy is a pursuit, and it is only in eternity that the striving ceases.

It was C. S. Lewis who said that "the Christians who did most for the present world were just those who thought most of the next. . . . Aim at Heaven and you will get earth 'thrown in.'"[28] We were not made for a fractured, sinful version of this world but for its redeemed destiny. And often the effects of the Fall via persecution, pain, and loss will absolutely shake our capacity to enjoy life.

Furthermore, in his book *Happiness*, Randy Alcorn states,

We'll be far happier in this life if we understand it isn't our only chance for happiness . . . and neither is it our best chance. I've read books on happiness stressing that we must be happy right here and now, living in the moment, because *this is all we have*. But the Christian worldview is that God's people will have an eternity of present-tense happiness. This assurance of never-ending happiness is capable of front-loading joy into our lives today.

In the ages to come, we'll remember past happiness and its cause (God) and look forward to future happiness and its cause (God). So if you're not happy today, or if your happiness isn't as deep as you wish, relax. Take a deep breath. You're not missing your only opportunity to be happy! The time is coming when there will be nothing you can do except be happy. And that time will never end![29]

It was "for the joy that lay before him" that Jesus "endured the cross."[30]

This is the power of the Christianity of Christ—in abundance or abasement, we take hope that our greatest joys are always ahead of us. Whether during the redemptive process or after all things are fulfilled, the good-dangerous Christians in this world can rejoice always, revel in the beauty of creation, and care for the spiritual and physical needs of themselves and of the least of these. And in doing so, be a people marked by joy.

CHAPTER 10
DANGEROUS SPEECH

A-K, A-K, that's how my tongue sprays, / Love is my clip and / Ya'll gonna be my gun range.
"HCB FREESTYLE"

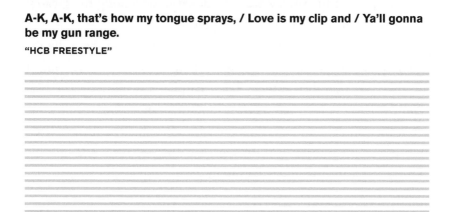

A few years ago, a research group called Musixmatch did a study comparing lyrics across a variety of musical genres. They looked at the vocabulary size used in hip-hop, folk, rock, heavy metal, country, indie rock, pop, and electronic music, taking into account the number of distinct words individual artists used throughout their hundred densest songs; the total number of words used in that same list of songs; and the average number of words used between each new, distinct word.[1] I know, right?

What they found was that hip-hop lyrics have "the highest average vocabulary size of 1,963 words with 478 words used per song and 94 new words per song." The top artists—across all genres, mind you—are Eminem, Jay-Z, Tupac, and Kanye West.[2] In other words, statistically speaking, hip-hop produces some of the greatest artistic masters of the English language.

This doesn't surprise me. Hip-hop artists are constantly bending syllables, reimagining phrases, and utilizing metaphors and analogies to bring the listener into the world of their experiences. They are audio authors or verbal painters, each word serving as a brush stroke, color, or hue. Those that do it the best are not only giving life to what they are feeling, but they are also giving us language for what we are feeling. This is why so many people find artists to be like distant therapists. It is no coincidence that the four rappers that hold the top spots in the survey are considered to be among the greatest artists ever. The point is, words are power.

I respect what we call mumble rappers—guys who basically say the same thing over and over again or literally don't say anything at all; they just mumble sounds. Their emphasis is more on the beat than the lyrics, which has its own kind of strange power. But more often than not the most influential hip-hop artists treat each word they use as a weapon to cut through the noise of the world and the culture to create a work that truly impacts people's lives. For better or for worse.

Now, consider that God determined that the primary way He would reveal Himself to people would be in words, so much so that the Son of God is called *the* Word. John tells us, "In the beginning was the Word, and the Word was with God, and the Word was God."[3] And Paul says that in Christ "all things hold together."[4] Jesus' title is the Word because He is the perfect expression of the thoughts of heaven. It was the Word of God that spoke in Genesis 1 and created everything, and that Word now is literally holding all things together. The term "word of God" can have slightly different meanings depending on where it's used in the Bible, but one thing is for sure: the words of God are the primary means by which He accomplishes anything in His world. Isaiah 55:11 assures us that God's word does not return "empty," without accomplishing the purpose for which it was sent out. The author of Hebrews tells us, "The word of God is living and effective and sharper than any double-edged sword, penetrating as far as the separation of soul and spirit, joints and marrow. It is able to judge the thoughts and intentions of the heart."[5] That, my brothers and sisters, is why I believe there is a uniqueness to language that is essential to understanding the Christianity of Christ.

YO, JESUS IS DOPE!

When I came to Jesus in 2005, I was ready to surrender anything and everything for the sake of knowing God. I broke things off with several associates. In fact, because I was a bit of a playboy before meeting Jesus, I even gave up dating altogether until somebody could teach me how to do it in a way that honored God. I graduated high school with a college degree, allowing me automatic acceptance into any school in Florida, but because I knew college living might afford too much freedom for my young faith, I went to an obscure Bible college to focus on learning the Bible.

But like the Christian rapper that led me to Jesus, I knew from the beginning that God was not calling me to cut off my dreadlocks, put on a three-piece suit, and walk around singing hymns all day. I was unapologetically Black, unapologetically urban, and unapologetically Christian. And to my surprise, all across Tampa Bay, God was saving and gathering young brothers and sisters that were as unchurched and serious about Jesus as I was. God brought us together, and it felt like there was a season where whoever came around this movement got saved. By 2010, our numbers were in the hundreds—a young, hungry, black, white, brown, yellow gospel movement we called "HGA," or "His Glory Alone."

Most of us were single with no real responsibilities, so we spent all our days and nights serving our churches, studying the Bible, and sharing the gospel in the streets. What was interesting was that we got a lot of respect from family, friends, and neighbors that were fascinated by the transformation they were witnessing in the lives of people they had grown up with. But there were some church folk that were very suspicious of what God was doing in HGA.

I recall on one occasion some friends and I ran into a group of Christians out sharing the gospel in the club district of the city. I was excited to see brothers and sisters out doing the work of our Lord, but no matter how much we explained our love for God and our enthusiasm around mission to them, they would not believe we were actually Christians. It was if they thought we were playing a prank on them. And there really was no reason for their doubt other than that we didn't look and sound like "Christians" to them.

They took one look at us with our baggy pants, dreads, durags, earrings, and tattoos, and they could not reconcile in their minds how we could love Jesus just like they did. They had no category for it.

Add to that the fact that we were all from poor communities, so we had a different vocabulary than they did. Ebonics is largely made fun of in the wider culture when it is simply a dialect of the English language. Though slang may not be seen as professional, it is not an indication of stupidity or godlessness. If our friends' standard for intellect and righteousness is the fashion and vocabulary of suburban white people, then of course we would look like imposters. This is why Black people often do what is commonly referred to as code switching—they change their tone, overarticulate their words, use words they wouldn't typically use, and leave out a whole world of words they normally use to "appear" more intelligent and approachable in environments where they are minorities. But because these were brothers in Christ, we let our guard down, and we spoke how we speak. "Yo, you know, man, Jesus is dope! I mean, God *rocked* us, you know what I'm saying?" And you could tell by the looks on their faces that they were thinking, *Christians don't sound like that.* This happened enough times that I started to think deeply about what a Christian *does* look and sound like.

Now, the Christianity of the Land has all kinds of answers to

What a Christian looks like has nothing to do with race, skin tone, hairstyle, or style of clothes, and everything to do with living like Jesus.

those questions, and there is certainly a racial dynamic. Even though Christianity is more thoroughly practiced in the Black community today than any other community in the nation, and even though Christianity is exploding in the Global South, it is often seen as the white folks' thing. Case in point: I've routinely been the object of suspicion at predominantly white evangelical concerts and conferences, to the point where I haven't been allowed in—even with credentials!—and am often met by a sea of confused looks and stares. And don't let me start talking! My choice of words is informed by my upbringing, and it has caused all kinds of disruption. My experience in the Black church has not been much different in this area. It has felt, at times, like people would be happier if I looked like church folks rather than acting like Jesus.

But, brothers and sisters, what a Christian looks like has nothing to do with race, skin tone, hairstyle, or style of clothes, and everything to do with living like Jesus—about whom, by the way, the Bible conveniently omits almost everything about his race, skin tone, hairstyle, and clothing choices.

The same goes for what a Christian sounds like. One of the myths of the Christianity of the Land is that English is God's preferred language and that English, articulated well, has some kind of correlation to spirituality. My grandmother, for example, was a spiritual giant, but by these standards, she would hardly be regarded as such.

Setting aside the fact that Jesus never spoke English, Christian speech is not about dialect or articulation. Indeed, as we saw, Jesus and His disciples were Galilean, and Galileans were known to sound barbaric and uneducated—in other words, ghetto. Granted, in Acts 2, we learn that when the disciples addressed the crowd, the Holy Spirit gave them the power to speak in a multitude of languages so that everyone could understand them, regardless of their native tongue. And yet the entire New Testament church was launched by the words of people who sounded ghetto. Let that sink in. Christian speech, as demonstrated by the original disciples, was not refined. So why do we insist that Christians today all have to sound alike?

BOMBS AWAY!

Christian speech is also not predominantly about vocabulary. A lot of people think that deliberately eliminating four-letter words from their speech makes it Christian. And yet, if you look at all of the devil's conversations throughout Scripture, you cannot point to a single "bad" word. Even though there were curse words available in the ancient Near East, Satan did not appropriate any of them in his speeches. Let *that* sink in.

Yet the devil's tongue is the world's vilest conveyor of evil speech. Indeed, the Scripture says that he has been lying since the beginning,[6] and I wholeheartedly believe it is part of the devil's tactic for us to focus all of our Christian-speech energy on not dropping f-bombs rather than God's purposes for all our words.

I'm not advocating for the use of f-bombs, but f-bombs are not necessary to tear somebody down. I was always taught that people who rely on four-letter words to communicate do so because they have a shallow vocabulary. Frankly, my experience has taught me that if someone wants to tear me down with their words, I *prefer* a shallow vocabulary. It's easy to understand, and the rant usually doesn't last very long. In contrast, it has been the verbose, articulate words of slander that have felt like knife turns in my soul and have hurt far worse. Indeed, I testify to you today that the most damaging exchanges I've ever been part of have not involved a single curse word.

I have mediated conversation between brothers who are in conflict and watched one brother completely eviscerate the other with passive aggression, false accusations, and gracelessness. Even nonverbal communication—rolling the eyes, deliberately looking away, and laughing—can completely destroy people.

A few years ago, a guy came to one of my shows. I was performing at a church, and he worked for the label I was part of. He was sent to "show face." Anyway, the show went well, and after it was over, he came onto my tour bus, sat down across from me, and told me—to my face—"Your Christian rap sound isn't relevant anymore."

I pushed back for clarity because there is no Christian rap sound. Country is a sound. Latin music is a sound. But as far as Christian rap goes, I don't sound like Lecrae. Lecrae doesn't sound like Bizzle. And Bizzle doesn't sound like Trip Lee. What he was really telling me was he didn't like the content of my rap. He was basically saying that me leaning into Jesus so hard in my lyrics made my music irrelevant and that performing at churches was corny.

So I sat there, and I was like, *We just had five hundred people out here in the middle-of-nowhere Texas listen to us proclaim Jesus for two and a half hours, some who came to know the Lord tonight for the first time, and this guy left that concert, walked past my tour manager, my road manager, my DJ, and my guitar player, came through a trailer filled with tens of thousands of dollars of production equipment attached to my tour bus—all signs of a successful mid-tier artist—sits down in front of me, and tells me it's all irrelevant?* Worse yet, he did it in front of another artist.

The brother has since apologized for his comments, and I don't believe he truly felt what his words represented—we are at total peace now—but without a single four-letter word, he brought disparagement on the whole tour.

Proverbs 18:21 says, "Death and life are in the power of the tongue." And since this is probably one of the most abused verses in the Bible, let me quickly establish what this does not mean. This does not mean that we have the power to speak things into existence. Only God can do that. We have to *create* things into existence. Our words are not magical in that the right amount of positivity or properly ordered speech can act as spells that make stuff happen (unless you're actually doing witchcraft). I have watched people I love refuse to be honest with their doctors for fear they might bring evil on themselves by admitting they were sick. Believe me: a positive vocabulary is not all it takes to get positive outcomes. It's more than that. But brothers and sisters, it's not less than that. What this verse means is that your words, depending on how you use them, can be the difference between life and death for those around you.

Jon Bloom writes that "Tongues can be weapons of mass destruction, launching holocausts and wars. Tongues can also be the death of marriages, families, friendships, churches, careers, hopes, understanding, reputations, missionary efforts, and governments."[7]

But this is the wonder of Jesus getting a hold on our speech. Powerful things that are used as agents of destruction, when used correctly, can become agents of redemption. True Christian speech born of the Christianity of Christ is among our greatest weapons in this world.

There is a profound moment when the prophet Isaiah is in the very presence of God. Smoke is filling the room, its foundations are shaking, there is a vision of a throne, and heavenly beings are singing songs about the brilliance and purity of God. It's overwhelming. When the prophet finally musters the strength to speak, he says, "Woe is me for I am ruined because I am a man of unclean lips and live among a people of unclean lips."[8] The first thing Isaiah addresses is his speech and the speech of everyone around him.

When we see God, we see our tongues, because our tongues are mirrors of the condition of our hearts. Jesus says that "the mouth speaks from the overflow of the heart," and James says, "If anyone thinks he is religious without controlling his tongue, his religion is useless and he deceives himself."[9]

Jesus further says, "I tell you that on the day of judgment people will have to account for every careless word they speak."[10] Judgment, according to Jesus, goes beyond the words you don't use to encompass the carelessness of the words you do use. You can avoid curse words and still be gossiping, tearing others down, murmuring, complaining, or simply being insensitive and thoughtless.

Over time, certain words become more or less offensive. Cultures decide that, and I believe that to use language that is appropriate for the occasion, we should consider each culture's understanding of foul language so that we might not be a stumbling block for those we wish to reach. It is appropriate to avoid certain words that, culturally understood, exist for the purpose of publicizing the wickedness in our hearts.

But we should not feel as though we have arrived at Christian speech because we replace four-letter words with G-rated substitutes. I'd submit to you that Christian speech is not primarily about what words we use but about how we use our words. Any word, as far as God is concerned, can be an instrument of profanity, depending on its usage.

Paul says, "Whatever you do, in word or in deed, do everything in the name of the Lord Jesus, giving thanks to God the Father through him."[11] Paul is reminding us that "whatever" words we use, we need to use them in step with the "name of the Lord Jesus." A closer look at the word "name" in this verse reveals that Paul is, among other things, speaking to the "the reputation of the Lord." We need to be sure that whatever words we use are lending themselves to the truthful reputation of our God. Indeed, the whole purpose of words is that they do not defile the reputation of Jesus.

Do you see why this is so much deeper than simply not using four-letter words?

WORDS WITH FRIENDS

I've got a pretty solid community. I've got my "apple of my eye" people—my wife, my pastor, my best friends—my peripheral people, and then my extended community. When I make music, I present it to a small group of people that I trust first. And then, if we feel good about it, I release it to the broader world.

I remember when I first started making music, a friend of mine made a song and turned it in, and the folks that listened to it were beyond brutally honest. They were like, "This is trash. What were you thinking? This could have been way better." And he was like, "Man, take it easy. I worked really hard on this."

Now, when I heard the criticism, I thought, *That's unnecessarily rough*. When artists get offended by that kind of feedback, they are seen as sensitive, too concerned about what people say, and unappreciative of keeping it real with them. But why does honesty have to be brutal? Part of the reason we struggle *not* to be shaped by the words of others is that we were made to be shaped by the words of others. Why do we think God takes speech so seriously? The challenge is not *if* words will shape us but *whose* words will shape us. When the Bible says that "faith comes from hearing, and hearing through the word of Christ,"[12] that's a community verse. My faith is strengthened or weakened based on what I'm hearing out the mouths of others.

THE CHALLENGE IS NOT *IF* WORDS WILL SHAPE US BUT *WHOSE* WORDS WILL SHAPE US.

As Dietrich Bonhoeffer says in his book *Life Together*, "The Christ in [a Christian's] own heart is weaker than the Christ in the word of his brother."[13] What I think he means is that hearing the word of Christ come out of people's mouths, directed at me, strengthens my faith in ways that just talking to myself cannot. You see that in the way Paul describes community in Romans 12. Paul tells us that we are to "outdo one another in showing honor" and "love one another with brotherly affection."[14]

Likewise, the author of Hebrews says, "Exhort one another every day, as long as it is called 'today,' that none of you may be hardened by the deceitfulness of sin."[15] The point is, it is not wrong to be shaped by the opinions of the people around you, as long as those people are God's people or speaking God's truth. We must take great care how we treat one another because our words have the power to push life or death.

A couple years back, I played at a festival called Rock the Universe at Universal Studios. I can think of few events that I was more excited to do. I mean, it was like performing the halftime show at the Super Bowl for me.

We were on tour at the time, so when we got to Universal Studios, I had my tour bus and my production team with me. When we pulled into the festival, we were like, "Man, this is it. We are here! Main stage. Universal Studios. Momma, we made it!"

> **WE MUST TAKE GREAT CARE HOW WE TREAT ONE ANOTHER BECAUSE OUR WORDS HAVE THE POWER TO PUSH LIFE OR DEATH.**

That night, we went on stage, and everything went wrong. I mean *everything* went wrong. For starters, the "click track," which is a metronome track in our in-ear monitors that keeps the beat and gives cues to us secretly, just decided to go public. Somehow the wires got mixed up and instead of the "1, 2, 3, 4" coming through my earbuds, it was playing over the speakers in the house. Certain songs came on with whole parts missing. My whole band was visibly rattled at one point, and everything just cut off. It was a disaster. In fact, it was so much of a train wreck that twenty-five minutes into my forty-five-minute set, I stopped it. Then I gave this little three-minute speech on how God is still good even though things don't always work out the way we want, and I got off stage. The whole thing rightfully infuriated the staff there. One staff member mentioned how something like this had never happened before. I profusely apologized, went back to my bus, climbed in my bunk, and turned the lights off.

I thought my career was over. I was like, *I just dropped the ball on the biggest stage of my life. Ain't no coming back from that.* Humiliated, I decided to go on YouTube to see if anyone from the show had left any comments.

I don't know if you've ever read the comments section on YouTube, but it can be pretty brutal. I mean, you get some of the angriest, most evil responses you can imagine. I'm talking people telling you to go kill yourself and saying they hope your family dies. Anonymity can really bring out the worst in people. Anyway, I ended up seeing other videos and began sifting through hell—I mean, the comments section—where I read, "KB is the worst thing that's ever happened to this planet" and a lot of other equally hurtful comments.

Then my phone rang. It was my friend Andy Mineo. We were both signed to Reach Records at the time, and he was calling me about a song he wanted me to do with him. I told him, "Hey, man, honestly, bro, I really can't talk right now. I just did a set at Rock the Universe, and dude, everything went wrong. Our equipment didn't work, I walked off the stage halfway through, fans were mad, I'm not getting paid . . . Man, it was a nightmare."

I half-expected him to say something like, "Awww, man, I'm sorry. Listen, I'll just catch you later, okay?" and then hang up. But instead he went on this fifteen-minute tear, detailing his own testimony of ball drops on stage. He even brought up my good friends and certainly one of my favorite performers For King & Country and the challenges they had suffered in the past. His point was that everybody fails. In fact, we are a community of failures. It's just that normally we do it in a less public way. Then he began encouraging me and speaking life into me, reminding me of who I was and of all that God had done and of what God still had for me to do.

I'm telling you, that phone call healed me. That night I wrote a letter of apology to Rock the Universe for what happened, and even though they didn't invite me back, I was at peace. Thanks to Andy, I felt like I could begin again. His words canceled the negative comments I had read online. They affirmed and solidified who I was, and they got me back on track. His words saved me.

Brothers and sisters, God gave us speech so that we might use it to minister to those who hear us.

We often call curse words profanity. *Profane* is usually defined as the opposite of what is holy or sacred. Indeed, James cautions us, "The tongue is a fire. The tongue, a world of unrighteousness . . . is itself set on fire by hell.... It is a restless evil, full of deadly poison."[16]

But the opposite of profane language is not non-profane language or neutral language but language that builds up. We are to constantly fashion our language in a manner where people are better off as a result of hearing it. Paul knocks it out of the park when he says, "No foul language should come from your mouth, but only what is good for building up someone in need, so that it gives grace to those who hear."[17] This is why the Bible insists on us speaking truth in love, so that even in our rebuke, people are not confused as to whether or not we love them.

LYRICS OF LIFE

Again, Paul tells us, "So faith comes from hearing, and hearing through the word of Christ."[18] God loves to speak through people. Sometimes it's a phone call from a friend. Sometimes it's a word of encouragement from your spouse. Words can be used to comfort, console, celebrate, and commemorate.

Most of my ideas for songs come from words I've shared with people in my community. Be it at church, at weddings, at funerals, at people's bedsides in the hospital, the exchange of our experiences via our words has shaped my heart and informed my music.

In many respects, my community is a microcosm of the world I'm creating music for, and as long as I never stop pursuing God's people, I will never run out of things to rap about. For example, I have a song on *His Glory Alone* called "Yes Song," which is a remake of a worship song called "Yes I Will" by Vertical Worship, and in it I say:

Let it all go dark 'round me
Hand in my face, I can't see

I have nothing left to bring
God Almighty, please
You have my baby
And you won't miscarry me
When it's so hard to believe.

One night I was with my fellowship group, and a dear brother was sharing with us about his wife's miscarriage. A father myself, I can't even imagine what it must feel like to lose a child. So as our dear brother in Christ poured his heart out to us, we did the only thing we could do—we loved him and encouraged him and reminded him that the Lord had his baby, and that no matter how dark things might appear, God would never abandon His promises to us.

Not long after that I wrote "Yes Song" as a testament to God's faithfulness in times of grief and despair.

The author of Hebrews says, "Watch out, brothers and sisters, so that there won't be in any of you an evil, unbelieving heart that turns away from the living God."[19] *Watch out.* Take care. Be very attentive. See to it. It is our responsibility to watch out for our brothers and sisters and to prevent one another from falling into "an evil, unbelieving heart that leads to turning away from the living God." Turning us away from the living God, brothers and sisters, is the sum and substance of the devil's work. The media has convinced us that devil worshipers, pentagrams, and paranormal activity capture the essence of the devil's presence. But more often than not, the work of the enemy is not that complicated. In fact, Satan's work in the Garden was simply asking questions. His favorite strategy is actively trying to erode our confidence in what God says, just as he did with Eve in the beginning. He doesn't want to just scare us; he wants us to stop believing.

So when the writer of Hebrews essentially says, "See to it that no one falls into an evil, unbelieving heart," he is calling on the community of Christ to prevent one another from leaving God. That's no small order. You and I, quite literally via speech, join the project of each other's eternal salvation. The words we speak matter!

I have another song on *Today We Rebel* called "Sing to You," which is about this woman who used to go to my church. Her name was Deacon Lynda, and she was one of the most on-fire Christians I've ever met. She was an older single sister, but she would host this event for couples on Valentine's Day called the Midnight Bistro. She would make dinner for married couples and just sit and encourage them. And she wasn't like this only on special occasions or with married couples. She encouraged everybody every day. A few years ago, she was diagnosed with cancer. Instead of this diagnosis diminishing her, her light continued to shine. She would come to church and worship and sing in between treatments with a joy and a love that was unmatched. Sister Lynda gave her whole heart to the Lord all the way to the grave, singing His praises every step of the way. After she passed, I wrote, "And Lynda, you had the heart of God / And until your last breath / Never seen someone seem so alive on their deathbed."

I wrote that because Hebrews 3:13 says the way we keep each other believing is to "encourage each other daily, while it is still called today," and brothers and sisters, many of us are wasting our days—even within Christian friendships. If we were somehow forced to stop encouraging each other to love one another and to love Jesus, many of our Christian relationships would go unchanged because we weren't doing that in the first place. We waste time speaking empty, useless words devoid of power and affirmation instead of breathing life into one another with words born of the Spirit. The Christianity of the Land would have us believe that foul language is the exclusive threat to our faith and uniquely hurtful to those around us, but it is not the words themselves that elevate or eviscerate. Any word has the power to heal or to hurt. What turns our words into weapons for good or for evil largely rests in how we use or don't use them.

Intentionally aim your words to strengthen your brothers and sisters in their faith in Jesus. Say their names out loud and pray intently about how you might encourage them to keep believing. Remind them what Christ has done for them. Tell them about God's love and purpose in their lives. Tell them about His patience toward their struggles and His grace for their failures! Defend them behind their backs. Go enjoy life with them. Sing good songs with them. Repeat good lyrics with them. Enjoy good films with them, reminding them that "everything created by God is good, and nothing is to be rejected if it is received with thanksgiving, since it is sanctified by the word of God and by prayer."[20] Praise them highly for their accomplishments![21] Outdo them in showing honor and respect, from compliments to tributes. Verbalize your love for them. Rejoice when they are rejoicing as if a win for them is a win for you (because it is)! And last but not least, tell them "I am sorry" when you have offended them and be ready to forgive when they have offended you.

Our words are one of the strongest weapons we have. Use them to be dangerously good for the Kingdom! Speak like your words are connected to the salvation of your brothers and sisters because, by God's grace, they are! This, brothers and sisters, is Christian speech.

CHAPTER 11

DANGEROUS SPIRIT

Filled with the Ghost, so I say what I feel.
"THE NAME"

In West Africa, I was blessed to meet a man that changed my life. His name is Pastor T.

Pastor T is a linguist, theologian, and local pastor. I remember Pastor T being distinctly marked by an overwhelming sense of joy, accompanied by the biggest smile I had ever seen. Pastor T was "that guy": sharp as a whip, committed to his family and to God's people, and when I met him, he was building a church next to his house so he could better tend to the needs of his congregants. Almost everything that left this brother's mouth was spiritual gold, and I cherished every moment I spent with him.

One day I was walking with Pastor T, and he started to hold my hand, immediately setting off my hip-hop-cultured, hypermasculine predilections. Because I was still suffering from anti-male affection syndrome (I just made that up), I had to remind myself that male

189

friends in West Africa often hold hands as a show of brotherly affection. Suffice it to say, it felt weird, but I bring it up because I distinctly remember setting my struggle aside as Pastor T recounted his captivating experiences of doing ministry in West Africa.

He recounted stories so fantastic, I'm sure you'd struggle, as I did, to make sense of them. He broke down the depth of witchcraft he had faced. He detailed the rampant poverty and its effect on the souls of his people. He talked about what it was like doing discipleship during the recent civil wars. He walked me through the implications of cannibalism and demon possession. He told me about the time he felt fear when he was called to pray for a little girl he believed to be possessed, who was physically throwing grown men around her house like rag dolls. As you can imagine, my jaw was on the ground. But without question, the most profound thing he shared with me that day was his assessment of how we do Christianity in the West.

He said in the West there is an obsession with only half of Jesus' teaching. There is an obsession with emphasizing teaching and preaching, but there is not a similar obsession with Spirit-filled power and demonstration, when both were present throughout Jesus' ministry.

"If you are going to do ministry in West Africa," he said, "you have to have the power of the Spirit." In other words, if you think you are going to roll onto the scene and talk, program, and preach people into a better place, you are mistaken. If you come to West Africa with a half-baked mission full of insight but devoid of power like the sons of Sceva,[1] the devil will have no problem running you out of town. You may be able to get by in ministry in America without the Holy Spirit, he seemed to say, but you can't do it here.

The truth is, we can't get away with forgoing the power of God when dealing with witchcraft because we can't get away with forgoing the power of God in any ministry. We are not getting away with anything in the States by not relying on the Spirit's power. How many more scandals, how many fewer baptisms, how much more of being

Is anyone looking for the unplanned, the unscheduled, the uncontrolled work of the Spirit of God?

on the wrong side of history, how much less influence in the culture will it take for us to realize that our witness is nothing—in the West or in West Africa—without the power of the Holy Spirit?

Pastor T was talking facts. If I consider Acts 1:8—"You will receive power when the Holy Spirit has come on you, and you will be my witnesses"—I believe Pastor T would agree that we often segregate this verse into excitement around being witnesses but don't think about what it means to have the Spirit's power.

UNSCRIPTED

When I think about the church in America, I believe we are excellent at representing who God is and what He does for the world in our speaking, our preaching, our teaching, our theology, our books, our conferences, and our music, because that's what we can control and engineer. But where are those who are equally obsessed with a fresh, powerful outpouring of the Spirit, revival, and deliverance? Is anyone looking for the unplanned, the unscheduled, the uncontrolled work of the Spirit of God?

It makes me think of the infamous words I heard back in college about the Chinese missionary who came to America on a church tour of sorts. When asked what he thought about the massive edifices, organizations, and churches he had seen, he said that he was convinced he had seen an example of all the great things people can accomplish without God.

He wasn't speaking to the de facto "creation power" of God, that literally nothing can be accomplished without Him. He was speaking to the fact that there should be something unique that happens when we're doing ministry, because ministry by necessity should involve the Spirit's power. I heard one pastor say it like this: "Our assignment is to invade the impossible—those things that cannot be accomplished without God."

It's a special thing that happens when the Holy Spirit is bringing people to life. It's not the kind of thing that can be built by contractors or orchestrated in well-planned Jesus events. It's not the kind of thing over-the-top church productions or some dynamic celebrity pastor can cause. It's possible to be drawn to Jesus-themed experiences but not Jesus Himself. The real work of the Spirit—people doing life together as a faith community to share in the fellowship of the risen Christ, to seek His will, to confess, to repent, to be healed, and then to be sent out to the world—is not brought about by earthly engineering; you need God for that. I've seen many churches succeed at putting members in the pews but fail at putting members in the Kingdom of God. You need God for that.

Despite the missionary's comment, there are large ministries that get it.

I think of my friends Louie and Shelley Giglio of Passion City Church in Atlanta and the multidecade-running event they do every January for college students. The gatherings they do almost always happen in arenas or stadiums because they are regularly facilitating some of the largest gatherings in the history of the church. One thing Louie and Shelley insist everyone knows about the Passion Conference is that it's not about the Passion Conference; it's about Jesus. Louie says over and over, "We've done well when people leave not enamored with how good Passion was but how good Jesus is!" Passion's staff spends days, weeks, and months beating on the doors of heaven in prayer, begging the Lord to step down when they meet. Louie has told me how they have intentionally guarded the stage, refusing to platform what I call "preachertainers," popular personalities that minister out of a sense of performance rather than conviction.

I've rarely encountered a ministry as resourced as Passion that is as committed to transformation as they are to presentation. The metric Passion uses to measure their ministry's success is sex slaves being liberated, repentance being actuated, Jesus being elevated, and young people being sent out to give their lives to the work of the gospel. The fruit has been undeniable.

But how often is the Christianity of the Land content with sensational gatherings and not the lasting impact of the power of God?

SPIRITUAL VS. SPECTACLE

In March 2021, the wildly successful rapper Lil Nas X collaborated with the art collective MSCHF to drop a custom pair of Nike Air Max 97s. Nike had not endorsed the move, and although they are normally pretty lenient when it comes to artists customizing their shoes, these shoes were different. The shoes were called "Satan Shoes," designed to celebrate the demonic. They were adorned with the number 666, upside-down crosses, and had what was believed to be a drop of real human blood in the sole. Nike sued both Lil Nas X and MSCHF because the collaboration had potential to damage their brand.[2] Predictably, this shoe that was an ode to Satan caused an uproar among Christians on the Internet. I say "predictably" because the shoes seem like a stunt specifically designed to trigger Christians, another battle in the culture war. But I think it's important for us to realize that rejecting a shoe dedicated to Satan is not engaging in spiritual warfare, especially since there is zero chance that any of us would wear the shoes!

I bring this story up because we are often blinded by the sensational. As real as the occult and demon possessions are, and as much as those dominate our imaginations when we consider what Satan is up to, that is not the locus of demonic activity. Most of us, beyond horror films, have never seen demon possessions, yet many of us think of our spiritual battle in these terms. Just because no one's head is spinning around doesn't mean we are out of danger. Indeed, Paul tells us,

> The works of the flesh are obvious: sexual immorality, moral
> impurity, promiscuity, idolatry, sorcery, hatreds, strife,
> jealousy, outbursts of anger, selfish ambitions, dissensions,

factions, envy, drunkenness, carousing, and anything similar. I am warning you about these things—as I warned you before—that those who practice such things will not inherit the kingdom of God.[3]

As I said in the last chapter, the sum and substance of Satan's work is to keep you out of the Kingdom. Have you ever thought of your selfishness, outbursts of anger, pride, lust, and jealousy as demonic? Just as packed churches devoid of transforming power can lull us into a false sense of security and distract us from the real movement of the Holy Spirit, so too do things like Lil Nas X's Nikes distract us from the real spiritual warfare within our own hearts. I don't believe spiritual warfare was increased by Lil Nas X's shoe. We were more likely distracted from the spiritual warfare that was already occurring. If we go the hardest against logos, brands, shoes, coffee cups, and Halloween, we run the risk of being distracted from the *real* battle, which, like real movements of the Spirit, takes place not on the stage or screen but in the heart. All of life is spiritual—beyond witchcraft in West Africa and ministry events in our churches—and the place where we need the power of God to tame the works of the devil is largely in the small, non-sensational "passions that wage war within [us]."[4] That is why in his second letter to the Corinthians, Paul tells us,

> The god of this age has blinded the minds of the unbelievers to keep them from seeing the light of the gospel of the glory of Christ, who is the image of God. For we are not proclaiming ourselves. . . For God who said, "Let light shine out of darkness," has shone in our hearts to give the light of the knowledge of God's glory in the face of Jesus Christ.[5]

Paul is saying here that the devil's chief operation in the world is keeping people from believing in Jesus. The devil's works are what blind

> **THE DEVIL'S PLAYGROUND IS NOT THE CULTURE WAR BATTLES OF THE DAY. IT IS OUR SPIRITUAL COMPLACENCY AND OUR BROKEN DESIRES—ALL OF WHICH THE HOLY SPIRIT WARS AGAINST.**

people from seeing the light of the gospel. That's the height of the demonic. The devil's playground is not Lil Nas X's shoes or the culture war battles of the day. It is our spiritual complacency and our broken desires—all of which the Holy Spirit wars against, provided we remain open to His work. As Paul reminds us, "Don't you yourselves know that you are God's temple and that the Spirit of God lives in you? If anyone destroys God's temple, God will destroy him; for God's temple is holy, and that is what you are."[6] The true power and movement of the Holy Spirit is that He dwells in His temple—us—and this is our surest defense in spiritual warfare.

WHO IS THE SPIRIT OF GOD?

There is an interesting Hebrew word in the Old Testament, *ruakh*—which is pronounced best when it sounds like you are clearing your throat at the end. (Go ahead. I'll wait.) It's the most common word for "spirit" in Hebrew, and it is used several different ways in the Old Testament. It literally means "wind" or "breath." I love that. Because if you think about it, wind is invisible but extremely powerful. It's a force that moves things around and shapes the world. Though you can't see it, it's obvious that it's there. Likewise, breath is the invisible basis for all life, vitality, and power in the body. Without it, we are nothing. Ruakh, when connected to God, describes the Holy Spirit, who is the invisible, personal presence of God in our midst, giving us life and moving stuff around. You can't see Him, but He is there working, revitalizing, energizing, and bringing things to life!

We first encounter ruakh in Genesis 1:2, when the Spirit of God is "hovering over the surface of the waters," patiently waiting to bring life, order, and vitality to an unformed earth that is wet, chaotic, and dark.

One of my favorite appearances of ruakh is in the life of my fellow dreadlock-swinging brother, Samson. Samson was out walking one day with his parents when out of nowhere a lion attacked him, and Scripture tells us that "the Spirit of the LORD came powerfully on him, and he tore the lion apart with his bare hands as he might have torn a young goat."[7] Think about that for a minute: Samson was empowered by the Spirit to rip a lion into pieces. A lion . . . into pieces!

In the New Testament, we learn that the Holy Spirit came upon Mary, bringing Jesus into this world through the virgin birth. In fact, the Holy Spirit empowered Jesus' entire ministry. Jesus, who was very much God, did not live His life primarily through the might of His deity. Paul teaches us that Jesus became a man—for real—setting aside (not losing) the God-ness in His fight to live a life pleasing to God.[8] Jesus was filled with the Spirit at His baptism. He was led by the Spirit through temptation. And after He died, it was the Holy Spirit that raised Jesus from the dead.

Then, in Acts 2, we read the powerful true story of the Holy Spirit being poured out on Jesus' disciples and bringing the church into existence on the Day of Pentecost. The Spirit of God rushed into a room where the disciples were gathered and waiting for what Jesus had promised—the coming of the Spirit: "Suddenly a sound like that of a violent rushing wind came from heaven, and it filled the whole house where they were staying. They saw tongues like flames of fire that separated and rested on each one of them."[9]

The Bible tells us that when the Spirit of God rushed into the room, He enabled the disciples to speak languages they had never learned. As amazing as that is, the power of the Spirit is bigger than the phenomenon of speaking in tongues. The power was in the content of the message the tongues were conveying!

Jesus, who was filled with the Spirit more perfectly than anyone who has ever lived, likely never spoke in tongues. Speaking in tongues was (and is) a means to an end, and the end is never intended to bring attention to the speaker but to the God who will use whatever means necessary to proclaim His Kingdom to the world.

Acts 2 continues with everyone present in this nationally, ethnically, and geographically diverse audience hearing the great works of God proclaimed in their own language, and the message was landing! Three thousand in attendance believed in Jesus and joined this new reality—the body of Christ. And joining didn't mean just coming to church on Sundays:

> They devoted themselves to the apostles' teaching, to the fellowship, to the breaking of bread, and to prayer. . . . Now all the believers were together and held all things in common. They sold their possessions and property and distributed the proceeds to all, as any had need. Every day they devoted themselves to meeting together in the temple, and broke bread from house to house. They ate their food with joyful and sincere hearts.[10]

The Holy Spirit's coming enabled the disciples' preaching and the church's unity. Make no mistake, brothers and sisters: Acts 2 is not some romantic vision of a church that was. It is the vision of the church that is!

KINDRED SPIRIT

The Bible is not filled with a bunch of mythological events that make for interesting conversations but don't affect our lives. Rather, reading the Bible for the Christian is akin to studying one's family heritage. God planned since the foundation of the world to redeem a people and connect with them not merely as servants but as family.

Families don't have to use neutral venues, buildings, or outside spaces to meet. We maintain our connections in our homes. So it is with God. No longer wanting to meet His people only through the Temple, priests, and holidays, God makes the hearts of His people His home, that we might have access to Him as friends and family.[11]

The same blood and spirit that coursed through the veins of your physical ancestors resides in you today. In similar fashion, the same blood that covered our spiritual ancestors covers us, and the same Spirit that empowered their acts empowers us. We are the Acts 2 church right now! Pentecost is not an exercise for us to observe. It is an experience to be lived!

The Spirit of God is the flex of the Godhead. God demonstrates His presence in power, and that power is in all who believe: "Now the Lord is the Spirit, and where the Spirit of the Lord is, there is freedom."[12]

What we have in the Spirit of God, who is described as our Counselor, Helper, and Guide, is lion-ripping, creation-taming, gospel-resurrection-bringing power. And Paul says we should pray to be filled with that power.[13]

When is the last time we fasted, prayed, or longed to be filled with the Spirit? Paul instructs us to ask God for this filling regularly. This is what we need! This is what animates the pure, powerful, momentous Christianity of Christ!

Let us for a moment appreciate the context in which God is pleased to pour out the power of His Spirit on His people. The first line in Acts 2 gives us a simple yet powerful guide for the Spirit-filled life. It says, "They were all together."

If we are to leave the rhetoric and step into the reality, if we are to be the Spirit-filled people who can live out that reality, *me* has to turn into *us*.

There is no one part of my body—hand, foot, eye, etc.—that alone constitutes my entire body. My body is my body when the individual parts are connected to the whole. The church is the body of Christ as it exists together as one. God's address is the gathering of His saints, and Paul calls that gathering the body of Christ.[14] Not that the Spirit will not fill us when we are alone, but there is a unique fullness about Spirit-filled life in community.

So should I go to church more? Maybe. But don't miss my point: we need a mindset shift in how we understand church altogether. If the gathering of the saints is where God is found in a profound way, it's not a matter of how much church do we need but how much of God's presence do we want? In a building or not, our question remains, *Where is God?*—because that's where I want to be! As A. W. Tozer puts it, "Every man is as close to God as he wants to be."[15]

> **IT'S NOT A MATTER OF HOW MUCH CHURCH DO WE NEED BUT HOW MUCH OF GOD'S PRESENCE DO WE WANT?**

Do we want to be filled?

PRACTICING PENTECOST

The book of Acts tells us that the Holy Spirit's presence was manifest among believers in three distinct areas: prayer, sacrifice, and teaching.

First, the disciples became people of prayer and gave themselves to calling out to God: "They all were continually united in prayer" and "They devoted themselves . . . to prayer."[16] If our prayer lives are empty, our souls will follow. We must do more than pray, but we have not done nearly enough if we do less than pray. Prayer is the first, middle, and last line of defense in spiritual warfare and in life. Committing to it is our pathway to the Spirit's filling and power. Psalm 127:1 says, "Unless the LORD builds a house, the builders labor over it in vain." We don't know exactly how our prayers and our actions work together—no one knows that. But we do know that they are in partnership—we labor, but the Lord empowers our labor to make it effective. It's clear that our prayers mean something and that through God, together with our actions, they have an impact in this world. It's like two sides of the same coin—we are praying, but we also are acting on what we prayed for, and God is the laborer in between.

We don't have to worry about if our prayers are perfect. Indeed, like Paul, whose speech and preaching "were not with persuasive words of wisdom but with a demonstration of the Spirit's power,"[17] we should rest our faith not on our own wisdom but on God's power.

And in the same way, the Holy Spirit "helps us in our weakness." When we do not know what to pray, Paul tells us that "the Spirit himself intercedes for us with inexpressible groanings."[18]

The disciples also became people of sacrifice. As we saw earlier, the church "sold their possessions and property and distributed the proceeds to all, as any had need."[19] Our spiritual ancestors in Acts were committed to love, and love necessitates sacrifice. Being willing to give what costs us something is indeed the highest demonstration of love. One of the ways we participate in this is by giving to our local churches. When you choose to give the money you've worked for, you acknowledge that, like your life, your money is not your own. We will never be richer than when we are willing to part with our riches for the sake of love. We might not sell all of our possessions like the disciples did, but if giving our money away prevents us from purchasing certain possessions, we joyfully join the Spirit-filled legacy of our spiritual ancestors.

And thirdly, the disciples became people of teaching: "They devoted themselves to the apostles' teaching."[20] And this devotion was not simply passive observation; it was active—it was hunger.

Where is the Word of God being preached? As my capacity allows, that's where I'm going! Where the Word of God is faithfully taught, the people of God will gather prayerfully. And the Spirit of God is not only poured out for our filling; He is presently empowering us.

The Holy Spirit's power described in Acts is indeed our promise. We *will* be His witnesses. Ask to be filled with the Spirit of God. Ask God how you might sacrifice for the needs of the people in your community. Commit yourself to regularly hearing the proclamation of the Word of God. If we were obsessed with just these three things, would we not be dangerous—the dangerously different, Spirit-filled, power-endowed people of God?

This, brothers and sisters, is how we practice Pentecost. The Spirit may not use the pyrotechnics of the upper room or the miraculous utterance of unknown tongues (though He could), but the power of a transformed life and a transformed world is ours in Him!

THE SPIRIT-FILLED LIFE

I have seen the Lord take men from selling poison to the community in the streets to literally flushing all their drugs down the toilet. I know a brother who took his massive gold necklace that captured his "identity" and threw it off a bridge into the ocean. I have seen the Holy Spirit take gangbangers, thieves, murderers, and racists and breathe new life into them. I've seen the Lord take the self-absorbed, the addicted, the abusers, the liars, and the dealers, and through His Spirit, turn them into new people. I've seen the Lord sustain the brokenhearted, the depressed, the doubters, and the lost through His Spirit!

I have a song called "Let it Rain," and in the first verse I say, "We see the dead raised here, another day at the office." That's what the Holy Spirit does. That same Spirit of God brought Jesus out of the grave, saved me, saved you, and is saving people all around us every day. Be filled with Him!

CHAPTER 12

DANGEROUS CHRISTIAN

Every evil in the world can descend against me. Not a hair will touch unless He decrees.

"HERE WE GO"

You can tell a lot about an artist by listening to their catalog. After the first few albums, an artist will typically settle into a consistent theme or style that in turn marks who they are. It's called "finding your sound." People might hear a song in passing, for example, and say, "Oh, that sounds like an Adele song" or "That sounds like something Kanye would do." A similar concept is when an artist "finds their look." It's been said that if you can dress like an artist for Halloween, their artistic identity has been solidified. That often corresponds with how they carry themselves outside of music—the things they talk about, their priorities, what they focus on in interviews. When an artist finds their sound, they often find themselves.

In contrast, there are plenty of artists whose catalogs are kind of all over the place. They seem to just follow the latest trends—whatever's hot. They haven't really found their sound yet. And a lot of times, that, too, can be reflective of who they are outside of music. It becomes difficult to pinpoint exactly who they are or what they stand for. Like their sound, they can seem all over the place.

Artistic identity has many parallels to human identity. Knowing who you are, finding your purpose, your life's "sound" means everything for who you will be in this world.

I can think of few more relevant questions to the collective identity of Christians in North America than "Who are we?" And perhaps the confusion around that question contributes to why so many of us seem unstable and all over the place.

GOD 101

Sometimes we overlook the Old Testament. Whether we consider it full of God's anger or long lists of names, we just don't pay much attention to it. But in doing this, we can forget that the Old Testament introduces us to God. In fact, the first five books of the Old Testament are essentially a cosmic introductory class written by Moses and presented to the newly founded people of God. The Hebrews had been enslaved for hundreds of years. No doubt their identity had become their oppression. Though they were a small and forgotten group of slaves, the Creator of the universe had said, "These will be My people." He then raised up Moses, who led them out of captivity and eventually to the bottom of Mount Sinai, where they would learn more about the God that saved them.

Moses begins his presentation with Genesis, which starts, "In the beginning God created the heavens and the earth. . . . The Spirit of God was hovering over the surface of the waters."[1] Now, the ancients were deathly afraid of the water because it was home to monsters and perpetually angry gods of the sea, or so they thought. So the fact that God's presence was hovering over the dangers of the waters— the waters He created—demonstrated that He reigns, even over the sea. Moses out of the gate wants the Hebrews to know, "This God

What the enemy wants to do is convince us that God isn't who He says He is and that we aren't who God says we are.

is more powerful than you could ever imagine. There was nothing before Him. He stands alone. He's so powerful that He can speak to nothing, and nothing obeys. When He says, 'Let there be light,' light has to emerge."

Almost immediately after establishing the might of the living God, Moses says, "God created man in his own image, he created him in the image of God; he created them male and female."[2] This God—this water-quieting, world-creating, sea-splitting, army-destroying, oppression-ending God—made you as a reflection of Himself. I'm reminded how my mother would say to me as a child, "Remember, you are somebody." Her thought was that if I allowed the subtle discrediting and condescending messages in the world to convince me I was nothing, I'd start acting recklessly like I was nothing. What would you want a newly freed group of Hebrew slaves to hear? "You are somebody—living and breathing sons and daughters of a mighty God!" Moses makes clear to us that the first things are first: this is who God is, and this is what it means for who you are.

What the enemy wants to do is convince us that God isn't who He says He is and that we aren't who God says we are. Moses knows this. I believe this is why the first conversation he has with this newly freed, systematically oppressed group of Middle Eastern folks is to speak to these two realities.

I am made by Him. His image is on me, and I am to reflect who He is to others. This quite literally is the most basic definition for what it means to be human. But the Hebrew idea of the image of God goes further than a status and speaks to a function. The image of God does something. In reflecting the good, kind, merciful, faithful image of my maker, I am healed and He makes me a healing agent in this world because I am in alignment with the purpose for which I was created.

This is the identity God desires for all of us.

If we don't know who we are, though, the devil will be quick to fill the vacancy with the lies told by our culture, by our friends, or by our own hearts, and we are destined to live out those lies. Identity is about knowing the truth about who we are, which is predicated upon knowing who God is, and then living in the light of that truth.

WHO IS KB?

I was eight years old when my mom told me that my biological father was not her first husband. It was very important to her that I had a father figure in my life—very, very important—so she married, admittedly in haste, right before I was born. Unfortunately, he ended up being abusive, so when I was two, she divorced him. But because he was there for the first two years of my life, I always just assumed he was my dad.

Several years later, she remarried—this time to a military man. Though things didn't end well, he was good to me. In fact, it's his last name that I have now. They were together for seven years, but there were some significant problems, so right about the time I turned fifteen, they divorced.

The insecurity of not having a father figure in my life and not knowing who my real dad was had a tremendous impact on me. I mean, a son typically feels cover from his father, like, *I can try to manage on my own, but if it ever comes down to it, I have recourse. I can go get my dad.* In a lot of ways—physically, financially, emotionally—your father represents security. And when he is gone, he takes that security with him.

Without a solid male role model in the house, I ended up turning to the streets to figure out what it meant to be a man. What I learned was that men fight, men smoke, men don't snitch, and men get with a lot of women. We see that a lot in hip-hop. Large portions of the hip-hop community would find it almost foolish for a man to be in love with one woman, married to one woman, and faithful to one woman. That would be considered bringing sand to the beach.

According to the culture, a real man doesn't show a lot of affection, especially not to other men, unless he wants to be labeled as suspect. The culture taught me that emotions in a man are not good. Crying equals weakness. Your status is wrapped up in your bank account, what kind of car you drive, what kind of house you live in—clout is identity.

It was a tough few years. And because I had been raised up North, I was a little more articulate than a lot of my friends, who, being from the south side of St. Petersburg, favored more slang. My vocabulary was connected to whiteness in the mind of a lot of my peers. I was called Oreo or coconut—you know, brown on the outside but white on the inside. I even had white folks that were way more hood than I was questioning my Blackness. So I tried to be Blacker. Even that had its own dynamic to it, because internalized racism makes you believe that in order to be Blacker, you have to act less intelligent, more ignorant, more violent.

We often forget that culture is not neutral. When we get on social media, go to school or to work, or watch a movie, we are flooded with ideas, each attempting to find residence in our identity—curating for us what it means to be a man or what it means to be a woman. And this looks different from how God defines it.

Paul says in Romans 12, "Do not be conformed to this world."[3] The world has its own mold, and that mold is trying to make you question, *Did God really say that was bad?* The God who knows you and how you work because He made you prescribes what your identity should look like. But there are a lot of competitors to that identity in our lives. So it is a constant discipline for us to answer the questions, *Who is God, and therefore, who am I?* That's how we live with our identity intact.

I distinctly remember my guidance counselors for the high school collegiate program I was in having high hopes for me. I had several teachers pull me aside and say, "You have promise." In fact, I was giving a speech in my college success skills class and mentioned my love of boxing, and one teacher publicly challenged me, "Please don't box, because if you do, you may injure your mouth, and if you injure your mouth, you will not be able to be what I think you're going to be in this world." I had all the encouragement in the world, but none of it was moving me. It was impossible for me to be motivated by the prospect of being a lawyer or doctor when I was conflicted about being KB. How could I know what I wanted if I didn't know who I was?

> **IT IS A CONSTANT DISCIPLINE FOR US TO ANSWER THE QUESTIONS, WHO IS GOD, AND THEREFORE, WHO AM I?**

Brothers and sisters, it is vital that we know who we are and what we stand for as Christians, because not having a strong sense of identity makes us susceptible to whatever viral attacks exist in the world. In that sense, having a solid identity rooted in God is sort of like a vaccine. It gives you the antibodies you need to fight the lies that threaten to tear you down. To live in this world uncertain of who you are makes you susceptible to whatever is in the air, and that can lead you into situations that are antithetical to God's vision for who you are.

For me, those attacks go back to when I was in kindergarten.

THE INVISIBLE MAN

My mom took great pains to get me into a "good" kindergarten, because studies have shown that children who don't start off on solid footing in school typically fall further and further behind every year and are more likely to fail. As it was in the '60s, the '90s, and unfortunately the 2000s, "good school" has often been tantamount to a predominantly white school. We lived around a lot of failing schools, many of them so run down and under-resourced that they appeared to the naked eye to be prisons. So my mom and a lot of other folks in our community knew that if you really wanted your children to succeed, you had to pull them out of the public schools—or at the very least, find them a public school on the "right" side of town.

I was one of maybe three Black kids in my class. Now, my parents had never talked to me about race. I didn't even know what race was, so of course I didn't know what racism was. And my family members were not Black Panthers. Most Black families don't sit around discussing *The Autobiography of Malcolm X*, nor are they daily talking about racial injustice. "The talk" about police brutality is normally just a talk, not a series of lectures discussed over dinner every night. This is not because they're not aware of it. I believe that many are just tired and eager to enjoy the freedom of being at home, where race is not a factor. It's also a tough conversation to have with children. I remember KBJ learning about civil rights in kindergarten and asking me, "Why are people so mean to Black people?" Suffice it to say, when I walked into my own kindergarten class, I was basically a blank canvas.

About halfway through the school year, I started to realize that there was something different about being Black. Now, let me tell you, I'm no genius, but I've always been a learner. To the best of my kindergarten knowledge, so were the other two Black kids in my class. Yet we were always given bad marks. Our parents were always told we needed extra tutoring. They were always told we were disruptive. They were always told we "just didn't get it."

We all sat at the same table. There were a couple white kids at our table as well, but the three of us were always seated together, and the teacher never spent much time with us. She rarely broke anything down for us or gave us extra help. And when she did get me extra help, she sent me outside the class to a tutor, who also happened to be Black. So even within the school, I was only being circulated among the Black folks. I was only being taught intentionally by the Black tutor. I was only around the other Black students—not because I chose that, mind you. I was a kid. That's just how I was seated.

Then after school, I would go home and turn on the TV, and all of the superheroes were white. All of the main characters were white. All of the leaders were white. All of the people who were important on TV or in history were white. So one day I pulled my mom into my room and said, "I don't want to be Black anymore. I want to be white." I was six years old.

Six years old.

Fast-forward twenty-two years. I was getting ready to go out on tour, my wife was dropping me off at the airport, and I was lamenting about how I was tired of all the microaggressions I have to deal with every time I travel. For example, when I pull up to the curb at the airport, the workers outside that help people with their bags hardly ever ask me if I need help. And usually, I show up with three or four large pieces of luggage. But they just look at me, then look right past me. Then they rush over to help the white businessmen. A white businessman gets out of the car and it's like, "How can I serve you?" I get out, and the assumption is, "Yeah . . . that guy ain't gonna tip us." After purchasing a nicer car, I thought things might be different. But nope. They still look right past me. I am literally the Invisible Man.

Many times I go to a hotel that my management team has booked on my credit card ahead of time, and I have to do everything shy of a blood test to prove that it's actually my card and that the people who booked the room actually work for me. I don't even check into hotels anymore. I have Sam, my white tour manager, do it for me. Just recently I had him call a hotel and say, "Hey, a tall, Black man with dreadlocks is going to be coming in with his Latina wife. His name is Kevin Burgess. Go ahead and give him the key. It's his card. I know it has my name on it, but it's his money. I work for him. So just look out for him, all right?" I have him do that because otherwise there's no telling what trouble awaits. The fact that I even have to *do* that is exhausting.

I recalled to Michelle the time I was running late for a video shoot in Miami and was going to miss the sunrise shot if I couldn't quickly pick up my rental car reservation. I approached the counter and was immediately hit with suspicion. The service agents mentioned that drug dealers had been using their cars, and as a result I needed to prove I owned a car and present my personal insurance in order to rent from them. Outraged, I cited the fact that I've rented cars for years and that this was prejudicial. They were unmoved. The other rental car company lines were too long, so I decided to stay and fight for the rental car I had already paid for. I grabbed a seat, went online, and had to read half of their company policy to find the section that said that what they were asking me to do violated their own regulations. I found it, showed the service agents, and then they handed over the keys—with no apology. I missed the sunrise shot.

Anyway, I was telling Michelle all of this and I just broke down and started crying, because out of nowhere, I flashed back to how, in kindergarten, all I wanted was to be good enough to go into the little treasure jar the teacher kept on her desk. It looked like a treasure chest, and inside it was a piece of candy, a bouncy ball, a yo-yo— things like that. And if you were really good that day, you got to open the chest and get a prize. I kid you not, every other student in that class got to go into that jar except me (and maybe the other two Black kids). I was devastated. That entire year, I never did anything good enough to merit a single treasure from that chest.

So there I was, a twenty-eight-year-old man, sitting in the car with my wife, tearing up over a yo-yo I was never good enough to get. I felt sorry for my kindergarten self. And the prospect of once again having to drag all my luggage through the airport by myself or getting denied a hotel or a rental car or enduring any number of race-induced frustrations suggested, apparently, I still wasn't good enough.

These attacks started at six years old, and they continue to this day. The world is constantly bombarding me with messages about who I am and what my worth is. And though I will defend my value, I am now at peace when others don't see it . . . because God does.

WHO ARE WE?

I see that the image of God is expressed in my Blackness because that's precisely what He sees. I see that my melanin is God's ideal. I see myself as an image bearer, where my value was good enough when God gave it to me, not when people recognized it. In finding Jesus, I found myself. There was a song we sang in church when I was a child. The choir would sing, "Whose report will you believe?" And the congregation would shout, "I will believe the report of the Lord!" This is Christian identity: a perpetual reifying of the Lord's pronouncement of who we are over against the falsified reports of the enemy. This is why the Christianity of Christ can lean so heavily into multiethnic realities. The "report of the Lord" is that every tribe and tongue will be present around the throne of God, singing "Worthy is the Lamb" in eternity; therefore, we insist on that happening in our communities now.

> **MY VALUE WAS GOOD ENOUGH WHEN GOD GAVE IT TO ME, NOT WHEN PEOPLE RECOGNIZED IT.**

The school that my children are zoned for is one of the most coveted schools in the area. Yet my wife and I chose not to send them to that school because it is so lacking in diversity. My nephew goes there, and he's complained about how his hair and culture are seen as abnormal.

My nephew is Hawaiian, African American, and Panamanian. He has this very rich, diverse background, and his mother is very intentional about making sure that he is living out the best of all of those cultures, but all of that is flattened into suburban, monocultural sameness at school. My sister-in-law is doing an excellent job in developing her son, but she is keeping him in diverse community outside of school because it's good for us to remember that not only is diversity the reality of heaven, it's the reality of this world. How do we prepare our children for God's multiethnic, multinational, multicultural world without those kinds of environments? To ignore this is to obscure the Christian identity.

Let me put it like this. If a bunch of men were running a women's studies program, you would, naturally, expect them to have some blind spots. Because while there are a lot of similarities that men and women share—the desire to be treated fairly, with dignity, and with respect—there are also some critical differences that would require one to have some kind of firsthand testimony in order to truly appreciate. There's a very big difference between what someone experiences as a native Hawaiian and what one experiences as a white woman in middle America. Our experiences are not the same, and if we don't intentionally think about that, somebody's experience is going to get ignored.

This is exactly what we see happening in Acts 6 with the Grecian widows. Scripture tells us that "the disciples were increasing in number, [and] a complaint by the Hellenists arose against the Hebrews because their widows were being neglected in the daily distribution."[4] Granted, it wasn't a deliberate slight. In fact, most scholars agree that it was due to the language barrier. But still, here you have the Acts 2 church—the greatest church that's ever existed—accidentally overlooking the marginalized among them. So what did the apostles do? They established a group of seven Grecian leaders to oversee the whole process and specifically remediate the issue with the Grecian widows. The apostles understood the issue. They understood the value and the importance of hearing and responding to the needs of their diverse community for the sake of the Kingdom. "And the word of God continued to increase, and the number of the disciples multiplied greatly in Jerusalem."[5]

My children are currently attending a charter school in the city, thirty minutes away from where we live. It's a tough drive, especially first thing in the morning, but it's worth it to us because not only does the school have a great curriculum, it has a truly ethnically and economically diverse student body and teaching staff. I love that our children are consciously being taught in the context of diverse communities. That is who we are as believers.

Michelle and I are building a new house, and we plan to engrave "Who Are You Becoming?" over the front door on the inside, so it's the first thing we see as we enter into the world. We want this permanent reminder not only for ourselves but also for our children, because while we can, for the most part, control the messages they receive in our home, we realize they are going to be bombarded with all kinds of messages we can't control outside of our home.

BE HUMBLE

Our identity is shaped not only by listening for, hearing, and walking with God, but also by being around God's people, meaning that our identities are solidified, in part, through the voices and opinions of those we are in community with. And that, brothers and sisters, is dangerous, because if other people help shape our identity, and the wrong people get into our circle or we listen to the wrong people, it can be disastrous.

Since our engagement with culture and in our communities prohibits us from blocking out the voices around us, we must develop reflexes or disciplines that make us discerning. One of the keys, I think, to staying centered in who God wants us to be is our pursuit of humility. The pursuit of humility is not being overly sensitive to criticism or overly dependent on praise. Ultimately, the praise that matters the most is "Well done, good and faithful servant."[6] You can get all kinds of praise from all kinds of people, but if you do not get that one commendation from the one who created you, the rest of it doesn't matter. But if we put God's praise first, above all others, we won't have to question our identity, and criticism will not sink us. It's not thinking too high or too low of ourselves. Humility makes us easy to encourage and hard to offend. The Christianity of the Land is often marked by hypersensitivity, being regularly triggered over the gnats of people not saying merry Christmas while swallowing the camel of ignoring injustice.

As an artist I know the temptation to organize my life in a way where my luxuries become necessities. Fiji water and 72-degree greenrooms start as preferences and then evolve into demands. They can become so much of my "artist identity" that I may be tempted to turn down an opportunity to perform at a jail or neglect consistently attending church because someone might ask for a picture. But while these smaller venues may not meet the world's standards of success and perhaps I will be inconvenienced by a fan at church, I've learned that is often where God wants me to be. And if I ignore that calling, I may never find myself around the very people I am called to make music for. I'll just find myself hanging around with other artists and other people of influence. If I get wrapped into thinking too highly of myself, I no longer am one of the 99 percent; I am basically a partner of the 1 percent. I won't smell like the sheep anymore because I'm just hanging out with shepherds.

This is why humility is so crucial to keeping a hold on our identity and calling in Christ. We can become too special. Untouchable. And when that happens—and we see that happening a whole lot in the Christian music industry—we fail to see that we're called to be Christians before we are called to be anything else. There are aspects of that calling that would lead us to love on people whether they can pay us or not, to lend our gifts and talents even if there isn't something directly in it for us.

We do have to provide for our families, but there should be times where that's not the deciding factor. We have to give ourselves to nourishing the true calling God has given us. And the true calling is nourished by not just following the cash but by doing things to intentionally remind ourselves who we truly are and who we are here to serve.

AT THE CORE

I'm a weird kind of rapper in that rapping was never my Plan A. I never daydreamed about being an artist or standing on stages or anything like that. Truth be told, I was planning on getting a master's in counseling and then hopefully working toward a PhD. But the summer before my senior year of college—not two weeks after I had decided I was going to give up rapping and instead help manage other artists I believed in—I was approached with a record deal.

It's not that I don't love rapping; it's just not the central thing at the core of me. I have friends that are like, "Man, if this music thing doesn't work out, I don't want to live." That's not who I am. That may be a little easier for me to say because I'm not a purist. But if your identity is cemented in anything that is not God, it will unravel and implode. What I'm most passionate about is impacting people—sitting across from a person and helping them figure out how to find healing, empowerment, resources, and wholeness. I remind myself that to be in step with my calling as an artist is to focus not on what I want *from* my audience but what I want *for* my audience. So if the music goes away, it will sting, but I will continue to do the thing I made music for—serving people. Helping, connecting, and influencing are core to my identity, and we trace those qualities back to God.

That is the universal calling I have as a Christian—to love people, to serve, to preach the truth, to empower, and to heal. The very thing that God is doing in the world! How that gets expressed—depending on the season—is a particular calling, or what I like to think of as a "local calling." All of work is to be a local agency of a universal Kingdom agenda. Meaning, purpose, and power in our work is found in bringing down the universal call into our local callings. Whether we are flipping houses or flipping burgers, our identity is nourished through our joining our particular work with what God is doing through the Kingdom.

If we can feel the gravity of joining God's work of sheltering families via real estate and feeding people via food services, those local callings are pulled into our glorious universal call, giving us joy in our efforts. One of the reasons we ask people we've just met, "What do you do?" is because it's hard to disconnect who we are from what we do. Though I agree with the maxim "I am not the sum of what I do," I prefer to say, "I am the sum of what God is doing through me." Because if I am ultimately joining God's universal activity of loving, serving, empowering, and healing, I *want* my identity linked to that kind of doing. I don't know who I am if I am not operating in my ultimate calling.

Rapping is a great vehicle for me to do these things, but it doesn't come first—it's not the whole of who I am. I can lose the rapping and not lose myself.

I'm reminded of the study that Amy Wrzesniewski, organizational psychologist and professor at the Yale School of Management, did that aimed to understand the intersection of happiness and work. She conducted her research on those that had the least desirable jobs, or "dirty jobs," as opposed to the kind of jobs you would expect people to be happy at. Her work focused on janitors at hospitals who would be responsible for cleaning up after sick patients. Her findings were nothing short of fascinating.

She identified two primary groups within the pool of janitors she interviewed—one showing contentment, meaning, and happiness, and the other showing grumbling, complaints, and discontentment. The difference between the two was shown most profoundly in how they described what they did. The unhappy bunch spoke in terms of the job description: "I clean toilets, remove waste, disinfect floors." But the happy bunch described the exact same job very differently. They actually didn't see themselves as janitors primarily, if at all. They saw themselves as "ambassadors for the hospital." One person said, "I'm a healer. I create sterile spaces in the hospital. My role here is to do everything I can to promote the healing of the patients." The second bunch was also known to go beyond the job requirements, offering deeper service to the hospital's patients. One custodial worker was responsible for the floor filled with coma patients, and she would change the pictures on the walls throughout the patients' stays in hopes the change of scenery might spark some brain activity. The happy bunch did not see themselves as holding a low-wage, low-skill, dirty job; they were lovers of people, empowerers, healers— servants of a great cause.[7]

Sound familiar?

Whether they knew it or not, this, by God's grace, is a strong example of the local calling being set ablaze by the universal calling that yields a happy identity. That identity can't be shamed by the cultural status of "what we do" because our identity is being shaped by our participation in what God is doing in the world.

My identity is secure when who I am is defined by how God has called me: to be a representative of His will, way, beauty, glory, and all the goodness of who He is in this world.

HEAVENLY FATHER

As a father, I use Father God as my rubric, my North Star to define the kind of presence I want to have in my house with my children. One of the reasons I strive to be a trustworthy man in my home is so that when I tell my little girl she's beautiful, she knows it's the truth— because Daddy doesn't lie. Culture will lie to her—I can guarantee it. But I want her identity to be shaped by the truth of the two fathers that love her wholly and completely.

The true tragedy of fatherhood is not when our children are unable to achieve a certain status but when they are not able to find healing, love, grace, and empowerment in our homes. I have a line in my song "Masterpiece" that says, "When you fall, baby, come to me." I have never written a line in a song that has made me cry as much as that one.

Brothers and sisters, we are all broken. We are all looking for a solution and salvation. We don't need to be model citizens to come to God our Father for grace. When we fail, there is grace for us. Is that not also true for our children? The same grace that we need, the same patience we need, and the same mercy we need—we need to extend that to our babies.

As important as it is for us to be working for our children's success, what is more important is that we are there for them through their failures. That's what it means for us to have God as our Father. He is constantly advocating for us to become better and become whole while being patient with us when we are still broken. And having a Father like that, we pray that we may be like Him.

I started this chapter reflecting on my father, who I had nothing good to say about until about five years ago. After my parents' divorce, he defrauded my mother, disappeared, and has refused to talk to me since. I have been abandoned by him for over fifteen years. But the Lord showed me that the grace I want to give to my children I also should extend to my father. I remember him for who he was, not simply for what he did. Accountability is another conversation, but knowing who God is has made me able to praise a man I struggled with for years. This heavenly Father of mine has made me a forgiven father and a father who forgives. That is who I am.

Part of what it means to have an identity rooted in God means receiving who God is in our lives and then expressing His character in the way we act as parents, as teachers, as friends, and as a community.

WE ARE DANGEROUS

Brothers and sisters, who we are is a reflection of God. And 1 John 4:12 (ESV) reminds us that "If we love one another, God abides in us and his love is perfected in us."

We are the crowning glory of God's creation, the cosmic chef's signature dish. That is our identity. It is not our status, our possessions, our social connections, or our abilities that make us a threat to darkness. It is the love of God that is realized in us and reflected through us onto those around us that makes us dangerous.

It's who you are. It's what you believe and how you live out that belief. The things you say and think and do can make you part of the problem or part of the solution—a threat for evil or a threat for good.

In *The Weight of Glory*, C. S. Lewis writes,

> It is a serious thing to live in a society of possible gods and goddesses, to remember that the dullest and most uninteresting person you can talk to may one day be a creature which, if you say it now, you would be strongly tempted to worship, or else a horror and a corruption such as you now meet, if at all, only in a nightmare. All day long we are, in some degree, helping each other to one or other of these destinations. It is in the light of these overwhelming possibilities, it is with the awe and the circumspection proper to them, that we should conduct all our dealings with one another, all friendships, all loves, all play, all politics.[8]

I started this chapter with the statement that our identity starts and ends with God.

People who know who they are in Christ, who see themselves as Christ's image bearers in the world, are the most dangerous people there are. They are imbued with the power of the Holy Spirit, obsessed with justice, with loving, with caring, with seeing, being, and fighting for what's right. They don't just memorize Jesus' commands; they lift them off the page and live them out every waking day.

Above all else, the identity of the Christian is love. Lovers are dangerous. That is what makes us a threat to the kingdom of darkness—to the things that might otherwise threaten the people we love, to the things that might want to impose an oppressive reality on our neighbors. Those things—sinful desires, hate, and injustice—can't exist comfortably in the world of the dangerous Christian, because they couldn't exist comfortably in the world of the dangerous Christ. It has been said that "the only thing necessary for the triumph of evil is for good men to do nothing." In other words, when good men do nothing, they become even more dangerous than evil itself. So, by striving for an identity that flows from our Creator, I become, like Jesus, a threat to the threats.

Jesus wasn't a big dude. Nobody looking at Him on the street would consider Him a threat. Indeed, it was His vulnerability—His ability to feel pain and His willingness to show compassion, to speak truth to power, to love, and to sacrifice Himself for the benefit of others—that made Him the absolute greatest threat to the kingdom of darkness. And by God's grace, we will follow in His steps.

We need a revival.

We need to love our God, our neighbors, and our enemies.

We need to sacrifice, to be filled with the Holy Spirit.

We need to empower those around us.

We need to live with joy.

We need to exemplify and expand the Kingdom. Indeed, we need to *be* the Kingdom.

We need to become a threat to the threat.

We need to be dangerous.

Let the Christianity of the Land die, and let the Christianity of Christ arise. It will, but will we be a part of the ascension?

ACKNOWLEDGMENTS

I'd need another chapter to recognize all those who deserve to be mentioned in this section. Thousands of hours of conversations, research, and experiences composite this work, and each moment of insight has shaped my life. I want to publicly honor all those who have formed me, directly or indirectly. Some names are remembered and others have slipped my mind, but the impact is permanent—this book is the sum of the people of God's contribution to my life.

I'd like to specifically name Michelle Burgess, my sweet wife who has supported me, counseled me, and comforted me more powerfully than any other human on the planet. Thank you to my brilliant literary agent Esther and to Proper Management for connecting me to her. I want to thank my pastor and my church community down in Tampa for teaching me the Christianity of Christ and nurturing my faith. Thank you to my *Southside Rabbi* podcast cohost Ameen "the dream team King mean machine" Hudson for being my closest confidant and friend—we have done theology and cultural exegesis together for fifteen years, and we are only getting started.

Thank you to my publisher, Sarah Atkinson, "the five-foot giant," for believing in me—literally finding me at a VIP meet-and-greet before a concert and pitching the idea of me writing a whole book. Your confidence and courage inspire me. Thank you to Isaiah Thompson for stepping in and allowing me to dictate several chapters after my brain hit a wall and I couldn't type anymore. Thank you to my senior editor, Jonathan, for your pushback and clarifications to the manuscript. Lastly, a huge thank you to Carol Traver for helping me bring this book across the finish line—I could not have done this without you. Also, "Look, Momma . . . I wrote a book!"

NOTES

FOREWORD
1. Hebrews 11:33-34, ESV.

INTRODUCTION: THE MOST DANGEROUS MAN I EVER MET
1. "Crowns & Thorns (Oceans)," track 13 on KB, *Tomorrow We Live*, Reach Records, April 21, 2015.

CHAPTER 1: DANGEROUS JESUS
1. Matthew 5:39.
2. Philippians 4:7.
3. The quotes in the following paragraphs are from Keas Keasler, "Ethics & Spiritual Formation," presented at Arise City Summit, Tampa, FL, June 23, 2018. They are based on Rodney Stark, *The Rise of Christianity: How the Obscure, Marginal Jesus Movement Became the Dominant Religious Force in the Western World in a Few Centuries* (San Francisco: HarperSanFrancisco, 1997).
4. Dallas Willard, *The Great Omission: Reclaiming Jesus's Essential Teachings on Discipleship* (New York: HarperCollins, 2006), 14.
5. Frederick Douglass, "What, to the Slave, Is the Fourth of July?" speech, Corinthian Hall, Rochester, New York, July 5, 1852.
6. Joel McDurmon, *The Problem of Slavery in Christian America* (Dallas, GA: Devoted Books, 2019), 288.
7. Charles Haddon Spurgeon, *The New Park Street Pulpit*, vol. 6 (Grand Rapids: Baker, 1994), 155.
8. David Masci, Besheer Mohamed, Gregory A. Smith, "Black Americans are more likely than overall public to be Christian, Protestant," *Pew Research Center*, April 23, 2018, www.pewresearch.org/fact-tank/2018/04/23/black-americans-are-more-likely -than-overall-public-to-be-christian-protestant/.
9. Frederick Douglass, appendix to *Narrative of the Life of Frederick Douglass, an American Slave, Written by Himself* (Boston: Anti-Slavery Office, 1845), http://utc.iath.virginia.edu /abolitn/dougnarrhp.html.

10. John Marriott, *The Anatomy of Deconversion: Keys to a Lifelong Faith in a Culture Abandoning Christianity* (Abilene, TX: Abilene Christian University Press, 2021), 23.

11. Matthew 16:13-16.

CHAPTER 2: DANGEROUS FAITH

1. Matthew 26:39.

2. Charles Haddon Spurgeon, *Morning and Evening* (originally published in 1866), https://www.blueletterbible.org/devotionals/me/view.cfm?Date=06/28&Time=both&body=1.

3. John 6:35, 60.

4. John 6:66, ESV.

5. Terry Goodrich, "Evangelicals Have Higher-than-average Divorce Rates, According to a Report by Baylor for the Council on Contemporary Families," *Baylor University Media and Public Relations*, February 5, 2014, https://www.baylor.edu/media communications/news.php?action=story&story=137892.

6. David French, "Do Pro-Lifers Who Reject Trump Have 'Blood on Their Hands'?" The French Press, *The Dispatch*, August 23, 2020, https://frenchpress.thedispatch .com/p/do-pro-lifers-who-reject-trump-have. See also Kaia Hubbard, "After Three-Decade Decline, Abortion on the Rise—And It's Partly Due to Donald Trump," *U.S. News and World Report*, June 15, 2022, https://www.usnews.com/news/national -news/articles/2022-06-15/after-three-decade-decline-abortion-on-the-rise-and-its -partly-due-to-donald-trump.

7. French, "The Pro-Life Movement's Work Is Just Beginning," *The Atlantic*, June 24, 2022, https://www.theatlantic.com/ideas/archive/2022/06/pro-life-dobbs-roe-culture -of-life/661394/.

8. French, "Do Pro-Lifers Who Reject Trump Have 'Blood on Their Hands'?"

9. "Induced Abortion in the United States," *Guttmacher Institute*, September 2019, https://www.guttmacher.org/fact-sheet/induced-abortion-united-states.

10. Tom Gjelten, "Multiracial Congregations May Not Bridge Racial Divide," *npr*, July 17, 2020, www.npr.org/2020/07/17/891600067/multiracial-congregations-may-not-bridge -racial-divide.

11. Gjelten, "Multiracial Congregations."

12. Gjelten, "Multiracial Congregations."

13. Gjelten, "Multiracial Congregations."

14. Psalm 91:2, 4.

15. John 15:14.

16. Daniel 3:6.

17. Daniel 3:15.

18. Daniel 3:16-18.

19. Daniel 3:28.

CHAPTER 3: DANGEROUS GOSPEL

1. Frank W. Boreham, *The Whisper of God* (self-pub., 2017), 8.

2. Charles Haddon Spurgeon, "Separating the Precious from the Vile: A Sermon" (United Kingdom: n.p., 1860).

3. Timothy C. Morgan, "Southern Baptists," *Christianity Today*, August 1, 1995, www .christianitytoday.com/ct/1995/august1/5t9053.html.

4. Evangelical Press, "Bob Jones University Drops Interracial Dating Ban," *Christianity Today*, March 1, 2000, www.christianitytoday.com/ct/2000/marchweb-only/53.0.html.

5. Anthony G. Reddie, *Working Against the Grain: Re-imaging Black Theology in the 21st Century* (United Kingdom: Routledge, 2014), 44.

6. See Mark 16:19.

7. Matthew 28:20.

8. Philippians 2:12-13.

9. James 2:18.

10. Dallas Willard, *The Great Omission: Reclaiming Jesus' Essential Teachings on Discipleship* (New York: HarperCollins, 2006), 61.

11. Matthew 19:21.

12. John 15:5, ESV.

13. 1 John 4:20.

14. Ephesians 2:10.

15. Matthew 25:34-36.

16. Os Guinness, *The Call: Finding and Fulfilling the Central Purpose of Your Life* (Nashville: Thomas Nelson, 2003), 157.

17. John 14:15, 21.

18. 2 Corinthians 4:4, ESV.

CHAPTER 4: DANGEROUS CITIZEN

1. Sydney J. Harris, *Strictly Personal* (Washington, DC: Regnery, 1953). "What's Wrong with Being Proud?" *Pieces of Eight* (United States: Houghton Mifflin, 1985).

2. Romans 9:3, ESV.

3. Jeremiah 29:7.

4. Luke 14:26.

5. "H. R. H. Princess Ka'iulani: 1875–1899," *Crown of Hawaii*, www.crownofhawaii.com/kaiulani-fp.

6. H.R. Doc. Public Law 103-150–Nov. 23, 1993 , www.govinfo.gov/content/pkg/STATUTE-107/pdf/STATUTE-107-Pg1510.pdf.

7. From Minority Rights Group International: "Native Hawai'ians still face higher levels of poverty, homelessness, unemployment, incarceration and ill-health, and lower levels of income and education, than the general US population. Native Hawai'ians also have one of the worst death and disease rates of any ethnic group in the US, and high rates of school failure, substance abuse, suicide, homelessness, welfare dependency and incarceration. According to a 2017 report issued by the US Department of Housing and Urban Development, Hawai'I has the highest per capita homelessness rate of any state in the US. Native Hawai'ians are overrepresented among the state's homeless; in 2016, 42 per cent identified as Native Hawai'ian or Other Pacific Islander. Dramatic increases in housing costs, exacerbated by the booming tourism industry, have contributed to this trend." See Minority Rights Group International, "Native Hawai'ians," https://minorityrights.org/minorities/native-hawaiians/. If you want to read more about the struggles of native Hawaiians, I recommend Haunani-Kay Trask's *From a Native Daughter: Colonialism and Sovereignty in Hawai'i* (Honolulu: University of Hawai'i, 1999).

8. Fred Nixon, "Donald Trump, Mark Driscoll, & Evangelicals, Q&A John MacArthur & Al Mohler Low," YouTube video, 6:28, March 23, 2016, https://youtu.be/TpogWiu8snQ.

9. Nick Givas, "California Pastor Told Trump: 'Any Real, True Believer' Will Vote for Him over Biden," Fox News, August 30, 2020, www.foxnews.com/faith-values /california-pastor-told-trump-any-real-true-believer-will-vote-for-him-over-biden.

10. Carol Kuruvilla, "Evangelical Pastor Defends Trump's Border Plan: 'Heaven Itself Is Gonna Have a Wall," *Huffington Post,* January 9, 2019, https://www.huffpost.com /entry/preacher-robert-jeffress-border-wall-trump_n_5c3640d2e4b00c33ab5f394b.

11. Emily Shugerman, "Trump's Top Spiritual Advisor Says Opposing Him Is 'Fighting against the Hand of God,'" *Independent*, August 23, 2017, www.independent.co.uk /news/world/americas/us-politics/trump-god-spiritual-adviser-paula-white-opposition -working-against-a7909401.html.

12. Psalm 146:3, ESV.

13. Isaiah 26:4.

14. See the following references: Jesus has one nation, His people (see 1 Peter 2:9). He has one political interest, His Kingdom (see Matthew 6:10). We become citizens of this Kingdom through faith in Him (see Romans 5:1-2; Ephesians 2:8-9). God's number one priority is His glory and the advancement of His Kingdom (see Matthew 28:18–20; John 4:34; 6:38).

15. Macey Lively, Christine Crudo Blackburn, *Poverty and Neglected Tropical Diseases in the American Rural South* (United States: Lexington Books, 2020), 90.

16. Philippians 3:20.

17. Matthew 6:10.

18. James Baldwin, *Notes of a Native Son* (Boston: Beacon, 2012), 9.

CHAPTER 5: DANGEROUS JUSTICE

1. Arloc Sherman, Danilo Trisi, Chad Stone, Shelby Gonzales, and Sharon Parrott, "Immigrants Contribute Greatly to U.S. Economy, Despite Administration's 'Public Charge' Rule Rationale," Center on Budget and Policy Priorities, August 15, 2019, https://www.cbpp.org/research/poverty-and-inequality/immigrants-contribute -greatly-to-us-economy-despite-administrations.

2. Michael D. Shear, Katie Benner, and Michael S. Schmidt, "'We Need to Take Away Children,' No Matter How Young, Justice Dept. Officials Said," *New York Times*, October 6, 2020, https://www.nytimes.com/2020/10/06/us/politics/family -separation-border-immigration-jeff-sessions-rod-rosenstein.html.

3. Quina Aragon and Maria Lerma, "Long Live the Champion: A Song for the Forgotten," *The Witness*, August 17, 2018, https://thewitnessbcc.com/long-live -the-champion-a-song-for-the-forgotten/.

4. Michelle Boorstein and Julie Zauzmer, "Why Many White Evangelicals Are Not Protesting Family Separations on the U.S. Border," *Washington Post*, June 18, 2018, www.washingtonpost.com/news/acts-of-faith/wp/2018/06/18/why-many-white -evangelical-christians-are-not-protesting-family-separations-on-the-u-s-border/.

5. Hannah Hartig, "Republicans Turn More Negative toward Refugees as Number Admitted to U.S. Plummets," Pew Research Center, May 24, 2018, www.pewresearch .org/fact-tank/2018/05/24/republicans-turn-more-negative-toward-refugees-as-number -admitted-to-u-s-plummets/.

6. Hartig, "Republicans Turn."

7. Eugene Scott, "More Than Half of White Evangelicals Say America's Declining White Population Is a Negative Thing," *The Fix* (blog), *Washingdon Post*, July 18, 2018,

www.washingtonpost.com/news/the-fix/wp/2018/07/18/more-than-half-of-white
-evangelicals-say-americas-declining-white-population-is-a-negative-thing/.

8. Matthew 12:34, esv.

9. Warsan Shire, "Home," Medium, September 11, 2017, https://medium.com/poem
-of-the-day/warsan-shire-home-46630fcc90ab.

10. Deuteronomy 10:17-20.

11. Luke 4:18, emphasis added.

12. Tim Keller, *Generous Justice: How God's Grace Makes Us Just* (New York: Penguin,
2016), 4. See also Deuteronomy 10; Psalm 146:9; Psalm 82:3; Isaiah 1:17.

13. See Psalm 97:2.

14. Micah 6:8.

15. Beth Moore (@BethMooreLPM), Twitter, December 9, 2018, 8:30 a.m., https://
twitter.com/bethmoorelpm/status/1071761110724960258?lang=en.

16. Job 31:22, esv.

17. Hebrews 12:14.

18. Leah MarieAnn Klett, "'Just Mercy' Author Bryan Stevenson on Faith, Death Row
Advocacy: 'No One Is beyond Redemption,'" *The Christian Post,* December 25,
2019, https://www.christianpost.com/news/just-mercy-author-bryan-stevenson-faith
-death-row-advocacy-no-one-is-beyond-redemption.html.

19. Matthew 23:23.

20. Psalm 116:5, esv.

21. Psalm 119:156, esv.

22. Isaiah 30:18.

23. Romans 5:8.

24. Bob Smietana, "Sunday Morning in America Still Segregated—and That's OK with
Worshipers," Lifeway Research, January 15, 2015, https://lifewayresearch
.com/2015/01/15/sunday-morning-in-america-still-segregated-and-thats-ok-with
-worshipers/.

25. Campbell Robertson, "A Quiet Exodus: Why Black Worshipers Are Leaving White
Evangelical Churches," *New York Times,* March 9, 2018, www.nytimes.com/2018
/03/09/us/blacks-evangelical-churches.html.

CHAPTER 6: DANGEROUS LOVE

1. See Galatians 6:2.

2. See John 15:13.

3. Matthew 22:37-40, esv.

4. Ephesians 5:2.

5. 1 John 3:18.

6. Luke 10:25-27.

7. Luke 10:29.

8. Luke 10:30-37.

9. Marian F. MacDorman, Marie Thoma, Eugene Declcerq, and Elizabeth A. Howell,
"Racial and Ethnic Disparities in Maternal Mortality in the United States
Using Enhanced Vital Records, 2016-2017," *American Journal of Public Health,*
September 22, 2021, https://ajph.aphapublications.org/doi/full/10.2105/AJPH
.2021.306375.

10. Brad N. Greenwood, Rachel R. Hardeman, Laura Huang, and Aaron Sojourner,
"Physician-Patient Racial Concordance and Disparities in Birthing Mortality for

Newborns," PNAS, August 17, 2020, https://www.pnas.org/doi/10.1073/pnas.1913405117.

11. C. S. Lewis, *The Great Divorce* (New York: HarperCollins, 1973), 118–20.

12. Lewis, *Great Divorce,* 119.

13. 1 Corinthians 13:1-3, ESV.

14. Ephesians 2:19-22, emphasis added.

15. 1 Corinthians 12:24-27, ESV.

16. James 2:14-17, ESV.

17. John 13:34-35, ESV.

18. Mark 12:31; Luke 6:27-28.

19. Jerry Bridges, *The Pursuit of Holiness* (Colorado Springs: NavPress, 2006), 120–21.

20. 1 Peter 4:8.

21. Ephesians 4:15.

22. Matthew 5:39-42.

23. 1 Peter 3:8-9.

24. Romans 12:21, ESV.

25. 1 Corinthians 16:14, ESV.

CHAPTER 7: DANGEROUS FRIENDSHIPS

1. Nick Tate, "Loneliness Rivals Obesity, Smoking as Health Risk," *Web*MD, May 4, 2018, www.webmd.com/balance/news/20180504/loneliness-rivals-obesity-smoking-as-health-risk.

2. "Loneliness and the Workplace" (pdf), Cigna, www.cigna.com/static/www-cigna-com/docs/about-us/newsroom/studies-and-reports/combatting-loneliness/cigna-2020-loneliness-factsheet.pdf.

3. Proverbs 18:24; 17:17.

4. John 17:21.

5. John 15:15.

6. John 15:13, ESV.

7. Genesis 2:18.

8. Ephesians 3:10.

9. Christopher J. H. Wright, *The Mission of God: Unlocking the Bible's Grand Narrative* (Downers Grove, IL: InterVarsity Press, 2006), 62.

10. 1 Corinthians 15:33, ESV.

11. James 5:16.

12. Genesis 4:1; Genesis 2:25, ESV.

13. 2 Samuel 1:26, ESV.

14. Sam Alberry, *7 Myths about Singleness* (Wheaton, IL: Crossway, 2019), 48.

15. 1 Samuel 20:4.

16. 1 Samuel 20:41-42, ESV.

17. Romans 12:10, ESV.

18. Ray Ortlund (@rayortlund), "You can be impressive, or you can be known. But you can't be both," Twitter, November 19, 2018, 6:16 a.m., https://twitter.com/rayortlund/status/1064477525093568514.

19. Amanda Smith, "If Church Is Supposed to Be a Family Then Why Do I Feel So Lonely?," *Premier Christianity*, July 18, 2019, www.premierchristianity.com/home/if-church-is-supposed-to-be-a-family-then-why-do-i-feel-so-lonely/1821.article.

CHAPTER 8: DANGEROUS BLESSINGS

1. Psalm 4:6.
2. Psalm 4:6.
3. Psalm 73:28.
4. Psalm 63:3.
5. Psalm 119:71.
6. Psalm 4:7.
7. Joni Eareckson Tada, *The God I Love: A Lifetime of Walking with Jesus* (Grand Rapids, MI: Zondervan, 2009), 302.
8. Charles Haddon Spurgeon, *"The People's Christ and Other Sermons"* (United Kingdom: Hodder and Stoughton, 1903), 293.
9. Psalm 34:18, ESV.
10. Psalm 90:12, ESV.
11. Matthew McCullough, *Remember Death: The Surprising Path to Living Hope"* (Wheaton, IL: Crossway, 2018), 59.
12. See Matthew 5:3-6, 10.
13. Philippians 4:12-13.
14. Proverbs 30:8-9.
15. John 16:33, ESV.
16. John 11:3.
17. John 11:21.
18. John 11:4.
19. John 11:40.
20. John 11:25.
21. 2 Corinthians 4:17, ESV.

CHAPTER 9: DANGEROUS JOY

1. Randy Alcorn, *Heaven* (Carol Stream, IL: Tyndale, 2011), 394.
2. See Mark 12:31.
3. A. W. Tozer, *Who Put Jesus on the Cross?: And Other Questions of the Christian Faith* (Camp Hill, PA: WingSpread, 2009), e-book.
4. See Ecclesiastes 1:2.
5. James 4:14.
6. Psalm 144:4.
7. Proverbs 9:10.
8. Ecclesiastes 8:15.
9. John 17:15.
10. John Piper, *When I Don't Desire God: How to Fight for Joy* (Wheaton, IL: Crossway, 2004), 182.
11. Psalm 19:1-4, ESV.
12. Psalm 92:4.
13. 1 Timothy 4:1-5.
14. Piper, *When I Don't Desire God*, 187.
15. Alister McGrath, *The Passionate Intellect: Christian Faith and the Discipleship of the Mind* (Downers Grove, IL: InterVarsity Press, 2010), 75.
16. John Calvin, *John Calvin's Bible Commentaries On the Psalms 119-150* (Grand Rapids, MI: Christian Classics Ethereal Library, 2009).

17. Frank W. Boreham, *The Uttermost Star: And Other Gleams of Fancy* (United Kingdom: Abingdon Press, 1919), 226.
18. See 1 Kings 18–19.
19. Dallas Willard, *The Spirit of the Disciplines: Understanding How God Changes Lives* (New York: HarperCollins, 1988), 75.
20. Willard, *The Spirit of the Disciplines*, 112.
21. C. S. Lewis, *The Screwtape Letters* in *The C. S. Lewis Signature Classics* (New York: HarperCollins, 2017), 221–23.
22. Lewis, *The Screwtape Letters*, 209.
23. Romans 13:14.
24. Nehemiah 8:10.
25. C. S. Lewis, *Letters to Malcolm: Chiefly on Prayer* (Orlando: Harcourt, 1964), 93.
26. See James 1:27.
27. Matthew 6:24.
28. C. S. Lewis, *Mere Christianity* (New York: HarperCollins, 1952), 134.
29. Randy Alcorn, *Happiness* (Carol Stream, IL: Tyndale, 2015), 408.
30. Hebrews 12:2.

CHAPTER 10: DANGEROUS SPEECH

1. Paul Thompson, "Kanye West and Eminem Use a Wider Vocabulary than Bob Dylan, Study Says," XXL, July 24, 2015, https://www.xxlmag.com/kanye-west-eminem-use-wider-vocabulary-bob-dylan-study-says/.
2. Emmanuel C. M., "Hip-hop Has the Highest Average Vocabulary among the Popular Genres of Music," XXL, December 4, 2015, https://www.xxlmag.com/hip-hop-has-the-highest-average-vocabulary-among-the-popular-genres-of-music/.
3. John 1:1.
4. Colossians 1:17, ESV.
5. Hebrews 4:12.
6. See John 8:44; 1 John 3:8.
7. Jon Bloom, "Fill Your Mouth with Life, Not Death," DesiringGod.com, September 2, 2011, https://www.desiringgod.org/articles/fill-your-mouth-with-life-not-death.
8. Isaiah 6:5.
9. Matthew 12:34; James 1:26.
10. Matthew 12:36.
11. Colossians 3:17.
12. Romans 10:17, ESV.
13. Dietrich Bonhoeffer, *Life Together*, trans. John W. Doberstein (New York: HarperOne, 1954), 23.
14. Romans 12:10, ESV.
15. Hebrews 3:13, ESV.
16. James 3:6, 8.
17. Ephesians 4:29.
18. Romans 10:17, ESV.
19. Hebrews 3:12.
20. 1 Timothy 4:4-5.
21. See Proverbs 27:2.

CHAPTER 11: DANGEROUS SPIRIT

1. See Acts 19:11-20.
2. "Nike Sues over 'Satan Shoes' with Human Blood," BBC News, March 30, 2021, https://www.bbc.com/news/business-56572245.
3. Galatians 5:19-21.
4. James 4:1.
5. 2 Corinthians 4:4-6.
6. 1 Corinthians 3:16-17.
7. Judges 14:6.
8. See Philippians 2:7.
9. Acts 2:2-3.
10. Acts 2:42-46.
11. See Ephesians 1:11-14.
12. 2 Corinthians 3:17.
13. See Ephesians 6:18.
14. See 1 Corinthians 12:12-31.
15. A. W. Tozer, *Tozer on Christian Leadership: A 366-Day Devotional*, compiled by Ronald Eggert (Camp Hill, PA: WingSpread, 2001), 23.
16. Acts 1:14; 2:42.
17. 1 Corinthians 2:4.
18. Romans 8:26.
19. Acts 2:45.
20. Acts 2:42.

CHAPTER 12: DANGEROUS CHRISTIAN

1. Genesis 1:1-2.
2. Genesis 1:27.
3. Romans 12:2, ESV.
4. Acts 6:1, ESV.
5. Acts 6:7, ESV.
6. Matthew 25:23.
7. David Zax, "Want to Be Happier at Work? Learn How from These 'Job Crafters,'" *Fast Company*, June 3, 2013, www.fastcompany.com/3011081/want-to-be-happier -at-work-learn-how-from-these-job-crafters.
8. C. S. Lewis, *The Weight of Glory* (United Kingdom: HarperCollins, 2001), 45-46.

ABOUT THE AUTHOR

Kevin "KB" Burgess is a Dove Award–winning rapper, speaker, and podcaster. With four full-length albums to his name—including 2020's *His Glory Alone,* for which he won the Dove Award for Rap/Hip-Hop Album of the Year—the multi-hyphenate artist is an inimitable force on today's scene. He has become a number one hitmaker and has received critical acclaim for his studio releases with placement on Billboard's Top 200 Album Chart and top 5 on Billboard's Top Rap Album Chart.

KB blends the creative and the pastoral with ease, having carved a unique space for himself as a hip-hop and worship experimentalist. His refined rawness conveys a kind of victory-lap energy you can't help but feel in your bones. One such example is "Church Clap," the bass-heavy rally cry that went Gold and helped cement KB as an inimitable force.

KB is cohost of the popular podcast *Southside Rabbi.* The podcast features in-depth conversations on art, theology, and current events and boasts hundreds of thousands of downloads per week across multiple platforms. Furthermore, HGA—a movement he spearheaded made up of multiethnic, urban men and women from all walks of life—has amassed a loyal following around the globe.

Although KB wears many hats, the joy of being a husband to Michelle and a father to their three children holds his heart and continues to propel him into the man God wants him to be.

Visit him online at whoiskb.com.

DANGEROUS

JESUS
FAITH
GOSPEL
CITIZEN
JUSTICE
LOVE
FRIENDSHIPS
BLESSINGS
JOY
SPEECH
SPIRIT
CHRISTIAN